Biblical Exegesis in African Context

Frederick Mawusi Amevenku
Senior Lecturer, Trinity Theological Seminary, Legon-Accra & Research Associate, Stellenbosch University, South Africa
Isaac Boaheng
Research Fellow, University of Free State, South Africa

Series in Philosophy of Religion

Copyright © 2022 Vernon Press, an imprint of Vernon Art and Science Inc, on behalf of the authors.

All rights reserved. No part of this publication may be reproduced, stored in a retrieval system, or transmitted in any form or by any means, electronic, mechanical, photocopying, recording, or otherwise, without the prior permission of Vernon Art and Science Inc.

www.vernonpress.com

In the Americas:
Vernon Press
1000 N West Street, Suite 1200
Wilmington, Delaware, 19801
United States

In the rest of the world:
Vernon Press
C/Sancti Espiritu 17,
Malaga, 29006
Spain

Series in Philosophy of Religion

Library of Congress Control Number: 2021936399

ISBN: 978-1-64889-324-7

Also available: 978-1-64889-176-2 [Hardback]; 978-1-64889-283-7 [PDF, E-Book]

Cover design by Vernon Press.
Cover image: Education photo created by wirestock / Freepik.

Product and company names mentioned in this work are the trademarks of their respective owners. While every care has been taken in preparing this work, neither the authors nor Vernon Art and Science Inc. may be held responsible for any loss or damage caused or alleged to be caused directly or indirectly by the information contained in it.

Every effort has been made to trace all copyright holders, but if any have been inadvertently overlooked the publisher will be pleased to include any necessary credits in any subsequent reprint or edition.

Table of contents

	Foreword	*vii*
	Preface	*xi*
	Acknowledgements	*xiii*
	Introduction	*xv*
Chapter 1	**What is Biblical Exegesis?**	1
	Understanding Biblical Exegesis	
	Conclusion	
	Review Exercise	
Chapter 2	**Textual Analysis**	7
	What is Textual Analysis?	
	What does Textual Criticism Entail?	
	Guidelines for Deciding which Reading is "Original"	
	How to Determine the Limits of a Text	
	Translating the Text	
	Conclusion	
	Review Exercise	
Chapter 3	**Contextual Analysis**	17
	Historical Context	
	Social Context	
	Literary Context	
	Conclusion	
	Review Exercise	
Chapter 4	**Grammatical Analysis**	25
	Word Study	
	Guidelines for Word Study	
	Morphological Analysis	

              Part of Speech
              Syntax
              Conclusion
              Review Exercise

Chapter 5   **Literary Analysis**   31

              Old Testament Narratives
              Old Testament Laws
              Psalms
              Prophecy
              The Gospels
              Acts of the Apostles
              Epistles
              The Apocalypse
              Conclusion
              Review Exercise

Chapter 6   **Socio-Rhetorical Biblical Interpretation**   43

              Historical Overview of Socio-Rhetorical Interpretation
              Framework for Socio-Rhetorical Interpretation
                  Inner Texture
                  Intertexture
                  Social and Cultural Texture
                  Ideological Texture
                  Sacred/Theological Texture
              Conclusion
              Review Exercise

Chapter 7   **African Biblical Studies (ABS)**   59

              What is African Biblical Studies (ABS)?
              Why an African Reading of the Bible?
              Historical Development of African Biblical Studies
                  Reactive and Apologetic Stage (1930-1970s)
                  First Steps Toward Inculturation and Liberation (1970s-1990s)

        Inculturation Hermeneutics and Contextual Bible Study (from the 1990's onwards)

        Conclusion

        Review Exercise

Chapter 8   **Mother-Tongue Biblical Hermeneutics**   79

        Some Key Contributors to Mother-Tongue Biblical Studies in Ghana/Africa

        Elements of Mother-Tongue Biblical Studies

            Study of Mother Tongue and Ancient Biblical Languages & Translations

            Development of Mother Tongue Bible Study Aids

            Interpretive Creativity, Innovation and Relevance

        Methodology for Mother-Tongue Biblical Hermeneutics

        Conclusion

        Review Exercise

Chapter 9   **Women and Church Leadership in Africa: Exegetical Insights from two Pauline Texts**   99

        Two Guiding Hermeneutical Principles

        1 Corinthians 14:34-35 and Women Speaking in Church

        1 Timothy 3:1-7 and Women in Christian Leadership

        Women in Leadership the Community of God's People

            Women in Leadership in the Old Testament

            Women in Leadership in the New Testament

            The Limiting Role of Women in Africa

        Conclusion: Responsible Exegesis for Contextual African Theologizing

        Review Exercise

        Concluding Remarks   *109*

        Bibliography   *113*

        Index   *119*

Foreword

...εἶπεν ἆρά γε γινώσκεις ἃ ἀναγινώσκεις; ὁ δὲ εἶπεν πῶς γὰρ ἂν δυναίμην ἐὰν μή τις ὁδηγήσει με; παρεκάλεσέν τε τὸν Φίλιππον ἀναβάντα καθίσαι σὺν αὐτῷ. (Acts 8:30b-31, "'...do you really understand what you are reading?' He replied, 'How can I, unless someone guides me?' And he invited Philip to get in and sit beside him"). I believe the words of the author of Acts 8:30b-31 attempted to show the significance of understanding Scripture passages and the agony of reading without understanding in context. How can one interpret Scripture without learning the art and science of biblical interpretation in context? In this monograph, Frederick Mawusi Amevenku and Isaac Boaheng contribute to the solution to the problem of lack of adequate biblical interpretation materials for the African context.

Generally, there are many books concerning biblical interpretation. The challenge is that they often do not consider the African situation concerning the role of the Bible in religio-cultural and social issues. Africans interpret Scripture within their context. In other words, the African person's experiences are brought to bear on the interpretive process/spiral.[1] Peter Nyende asserted that Africans read/interpret the Bible circumstantially. They approach the Bible with existential problems seeking solutions.[2] "....the Bible is not a book on the same level with books on the economy, geography or, agriculture, but a divine book which can be used [interpreted] to cause desirable change by those who subscribe to its tenets."[3] However, George Ossom-Batsa argued that, until the 1960s, biblical interpretation in Ghana was performed according to western conventions, which do not adequately consider the African worldview.[4] It implies that although there were many activities in Africa in the first century concerning biblical interpretation—such as the continent being referred to as

---

[1] Daniel Nii Aboagye Aryeh, "Contemporary Hermeneutics: An Examination of Selected Works of John D. K. Ekem on Mother Tongue Biblical," *The Journal of Inductive Biblical Studies* 4/2 (2017):182–210.

[2] Peter Nyende, "Addressing Ethnicity Via Biblical Studies: A Task of African Biblical Scholarship," *Neotestamentica*, Vol. 44, No. 1 (2010): 122-139.

[3] Daniel Nii Aboagye Aryeh, "Inductive Biblical Interpretation and Mother-Tongue Biblical Hermeneutics: A Proposal for Pentecostal/Charismatic Ministries in Ghana Today," *The Journal of Inductive Biblical Studies* 3/2(2016):140-60.

[4] George Ossom-Batsa, "African Interpretation of the Bible in Communicative Perspective," *Ghana Bulletin of Theology* 2 (2007): 91–104.

the cradle of biblical interpretation/translation[5]—the African worldview was not critically taken in the interpretation process.

Rev. Dr Frederick M. Amevenku and Rev. Isaac Boaheng have identified and agreed with other scholars on the critical issue of biblical interpretation in the African context and decided to contribute to the solution in this monograph because there can hardly be a universalist approach to biblical interpretation. J. N. K. Mugambi offers that "[h]ermeneutics, as a critical discipline, should help us to distinguish between the essential message of the gospel and the cultural gap in which it must necessarily be clothed from time to time and from place to place."[6] Amevenku and Boaheng discuss ways, means, and principles for interpreting the Bible in order to make it more relevant in the African context.

The uniqueness of the book *Biblical Exegesis in African Context* is that: (i) the language used is plain, simple, and well paragraphed so that non-theologically educated clergy and individuals can understand and apply the principles for interpreting any genre in the Bible. It avoids the many technical jargons that accompany books on biblical interpretation and limits it to a few experts in the field; (ii) the authors bring together various methods and approaches to biblical interpretation such as African Biblical Studies and Mother-Tongue Biblical Hermeneutics, propounded by African scholars, and Socio-Rhetorical Interpretation propounded by a non-African with the traditional textual, literary, contextual, and grammatical analysis in one volume. The book does not limit the discussion of issues to African scholars only. The adoption of Socio-Rhetorical Interpretation for the African context is insightful. The discussion of issues is very critical, so new and revised modes are suggested;[7] (iii) the principles for interpreting various genres of the Bible signify the uniqueness of interpreting each genre distinctively. The book has the potential of guiding and motivating students (both graduates and undergraduates) into areas of biblical interpretation they would like to specialize in; and (iv) the last chapter serves as an example of what was discussed in previous chapters and how it can be applied to interpreting Pauline passages. The book demonstrates the use of the Greek text, the way it

---

[5] John D. K. Ekem, *Early Scriptures of the Gold Coast (Ghana): the Historical, Linguistic, and Theological Settings of the Gã, Twi, Mfantse, and Ewe Bibles* (Manchester: St. Jerome Publishing, 2011), 2.
[6] J. N. K. Mugambi, "Foundation for the African Approach to Biblical Hermeneutics," in *Interpreting the New Testament in Africa*, ed. Mary N. Getui, Tinyiko Maluleke and Justin Ukpong (Nairobi, Kenya: Acton Publishers, 2001), 20.
[7] Frederick M. Amevenku and Isaac Boaheng, *Biblical Exegesis in African Context* (Delaware: Vernon Press, 2021), 82-84.

resonates in the *Akan* and *Ewe* contexts of Ghana/Africa, and how the message can be appropriated. It agrees with Aloo Osotsi Mojola's proposition that African biblical scholars should be able to use their native languages, history and culture, and the biblical languages in interpreting the Bible.[8] This would motivate students and the clergy to study their native/mother-tongue languages along with the study of the biblical languages.

The book contributes to solving one of the problems of biblical interpretation/studies in the African context identified by Emmanuel A. Obeng as the lack of reference materials that resonate with the African context.[9] Although the book can be used by other groups that share a similar ethos with the African context, no doubt, the monograph critically considers the African worldview concerning the use of the Bible and how its appropriate interpretation can help solve African challenges.

The exercise at the end of each chapter emphasizes the fact that it is a textbook that can be used to teach biblical interpretation in Seminaries, Departments of Religious Studies, and Bible Schools in Africa. The exercises would help the reader attempt to recall the main points of the issues discussed in the chapter.

Rev. Dr Amevenku and Rev. Boaheng have thoroughly examined the complex issue of biblical interpretation in the African context. They have given attention to acute details for biblical interpretation in the African context. The treatments of issues are characterized by a strong sense of making the Bible speak to existential issues in Africa through appropriate interpretation. As African Christianity continues to be very significant in the study of the faith, this book is timely. It is indispensable for persons who seek to interpret the Bible and make it more significant to Africans in their context. Rev. Dr Amevenku and Rev. Boaheng have fulfilled one of the elements of "righteousness" in academia by writing this book. It is our duty to read and apply the principles.

Rev. Dr Daniel Nii Aboagye Aryeh, PhD
Acting Rector
Perez University College

---

[8] Aloo Osotsi Mojola, "Outstanding Challenges for Contemporary Bible Translation and Interpretation in Africa," *Journal of African Christian Thought* 10 (2007): 31–37.
[9] Emmanuel A. Obeng, "Emerging Concerns for Biblical Scholarship in Ghana," in *Interpreting the New Testament in Africa*, ed. Mary N. Getui, Tinyiko Maluleke and Justin Ukpong (Nairobi: Acton Publishers, 2001), 31–41.

Preface

How can the Church in Africa affirm its uniqueness (in terms of the African identity and experiences) and at the same time remain faithful to the gospel message? The answer to this question is critical in African Christianity because of the many struggles African converts go through in remaining African and Christian at the same time. *Biblical Exegesis in African Context* has been published to guide African readers on how they can interpret the Bible within the socio-cultural context of Africa and apply it appropriately to their lives.

The book is organized into eight chapters, the first serving as a general introduction to the subject matter. After explaining exegesis and hermeneutics, the chapter sets the agenda for the rest of the book. The next chapter briefly discusses textual criticism, the task of determining the originality of a biblical text. It is argued that exegesis based on a wrong text is bound to be faulty and hence the exegete's first concern should be to determine the original text. Another important thing this chapter does is to equip the reader to determine the limits of a chosen text and provide a workable translation.

In chapter three, we consider issues related to the context of the text. Two types of contexts, namely, historical and literary contexts are discussed. After a critical examination of the various aspects of what constitutes context, the chapter concludes that contextual analysis is an indispensable tool in biblical exegesis. The study then moves on to examine the role grammar plays in one's understanding of scripture. Four aspects of grammatical analysis, namely, lexicology (the meaning of words), morphology (the form of words), grammatical function of words (parts of speech), and syntax (the relationships of words) are examined.

The book then proceeds to present and comment on various literary forms present in the Bible, prominent among them being, Narrative, Law, Poetry, Prophecy, Wisdom Literature, Gospels, Acts of the Apostles, Epistles and Revelation. It is noted that apart from general principles of exegesis, various literary genres require specific principles that must be mastered and applied. We dedicate the next chapter to discussions on socio-rhetorical interpretation, a recently developed interpretative grid which makes use of data from various fields such as linguistics (inner texture), literary comparative studies (intertexture), social and historical studies (social and cultural texture), ideological studies (ideological texture) and theology (theological/sacred texture) to analyze a text.

The next two chapters of the book explain matters solely related to the context of Africa. This part is intended to equip readers to interpret the Bible from African cultural perspectives and then apply the gospel message meaningfully to the life of African Christians. Chapter seven deals with the emergence and historical development of African Biblical Studies, (ABS), noting its relevance and how Africans can benefit from it. The main contention of the chapter is that Africans will better understand and apply God's word to their lives if they read the scriptures in an African way. The eighth chapter looks at how African languages can be used in deriving meaning of scripture and applying it to real-life situations. Here, the book considers the historical development of Mother-Tongue Biblical Hermeneutics (MTBH), the major contributors to this method as well as the principles involved in the approach. The authors contribute to the development of MTBH by developing a methodological framework for the mother-tongue approach.

The last chapter addresses the issue of the role of women in African Christianity. The question of the legitimacy of women leadership in the Christian Church is of major concern in the African society because of patriarchal dominance in Africa. The chapter contends that God calls all manner of people into Christian ministry therefore women must be given equal opportunity as men to perform any role for which God has called them.

We have the conviction that God wants us to use this book to help equip Christians, especially those faced with African realities, to better understand and apply God's word. This book is written in such a way as to facilitate use by both ordinary readers as well as scholars. Each chapter ends with self-assessment questions that enable the reader to have a deep reflection on what was covered in the chapter in question.

Frederick Mawusi Amevenku
Isaac Boaheng
May 2021

Acknowledgements

The task of publishing this book was accomplished through the efforts of many individuals who need to be appreciated. Though so many people contributed in their special ways toward the completion of this work, we take the sole responsibility for any shortfall(s) found in the book. Our highest appreciation goes to the Triune God, who has given us the opportunity to study his word and to write this book. We are also indebted to many scholars whose works we consulted in preparing the manuscript.

We are extremely grateful to our families, friends and colleagues in the various institutions in which we serve for the impact of their interactions and help to the process of writing this book. We thank Rev. Dr. Daniel Nii Aboagye Aryeh for writing a foreword to the book. Prof. Aloo O. Mojola and Prof. JDK Ekem are appreciated for their mentoring role in our academic careers. To the staff of Vernon Press, we say God richly bless you. Amen!

Dedication

We dedicate this book to all African biblical scholars.

Introduction

Africa has been credited for contributing remarkably to global Christianity in the 21st century. Africans have embraced Christianity in such a way that the Christian gospel no longer sounds foreign to Africans as it was in the past. Yet, the African Church still battles with the question of how best the gospel message can be rendered more meaningfully and practically to Africans. Since the survival of Christianity and the practice of authentic Christian values in Africa depend greatly on how Africans accept the gospel and make it part of their existence, African theologians continue to make efforts to contextualize the Christian faith meaningfully and relevantly to the African continent. A key question in the discussion is: How can the Church in Africa affirm its uniqueness (in terms of the African identity and experiences) and at the same time remain faithful to the gospel message? In other words, how can African converts remain both Christians and Africans at the same time?

Over the years various African scholars have grappled with these questions and yet have not reached a consensus. Issues such as polygamy, poverty, HIV/AIDS, use of alcohol, divorce and remarriage, homosexuality, cohabitation, and the like continue to exercise African theologians. However, in most cases, the approach used is based on Western frameworks. The need for exegetical framework that equips the Africans to read and apply the Bible to their life situation therefore remains with us. This study contributes to the discussion by proposing an exegetical method by which African Christians can interpret Scriptures for the contemporary (African) society (in terms of existential issues such as abject poverty, hunger, ethnic tensions, child abuse, corrupt leadership, war, terrible illnesses and all sorts of unpleasant realities).

We have written this book as our modest attempt to help Africans to appreciate God's word within their own cultural settings. Each chapter can be studied on its own. However, all the chapters come together to form the complete hermeneutical framework for interpreting Scriptures for an African setting. Most of the chapters examine elements of biblical interpretation that have been developed through Western scholarship. Some of them include textual analysis, socio-rhetorical interpretation, contextual analysis and others. We believe that these elements serve as foundational principles upon which African biblical interpretation can be built. We therefore considered these elements and later focused on African peculiarities. One of the key contributions of this volume is our attempt to provide a hermeneutical framework for African Mother-Tongue Biblical Hermeneutics. This area of research has been discussed by many African scholars without a well-developed methodology. The methodology provided in this study and the applications given under each aspect of the methodology will serve as a foundation for African biblical interpretation.

Chapter 1

What is Biblical Exegesis?

This study serves as an introductory material for those interested in Biblical Exegesis. It is intended to develop an approach to biblical exegesis that suits the context of Africa. The present chapter, which serves as a general introduction to the entire study, deals with preliminary issues related to the subject matter, including what biblical exegesis is, what it entails and why it is relevant for the Christian communities in Africa.

Understanding Biblical Exegesis

Exegesis derives from the Greek word *exegeomai* which means "to lead out of." In relation to texts, exegesis means "reading out" or "explaining the meaning" of texts. Exegesis is not strictly for professionals. Our daily lives require exegesis of one form or the other. We do exegesis anytime we read or hear audible sound and try to derive some understanding from it. By way of definition, exegesis is an interactive process of interpretation in which readers seek the meaning of the text in its original context.[1] Biblical exegesis refers to the process of arriving at the meaning of biblical text through historical/cultural, grammatical, rhetorical, and religious analyses (or through any other means deemed fit for the context in which the exegete is working). Biblical exegesis therefore answers the question, "What did the biblical author mean in his original context?" When the answer to this question is found, the exegete moves on to apply it to life situations in his/her context. This task of applying the results of exegesis to contemporary contexts is what we refer to as **hermeneutics**. Hermeneutics refers to the theories, methods, and principles of biblical interpretation, while "exegesis" refers to the act of interpretation. To use the words of Anthony C. Thiselton, hermeneutics "explores how we read, understand, and handle texts, especially those written in another time or in another context of life from our own."[2] Such an exercise may integrate a number of academic disciplines including philosophy, theology, linguistics, sociology, science and anthropology.

---

[1] Lucretia Yaghjian, *Writing Theology Well: A Rhetoric for Theological and Biblical Writers* (New York: Continuum, 2008), 146-147.
[2] Anthony C Thiselton, *Hermeneutics: An introduction* (Grand Rapids, MI: W.B. Eerdmans, 2009), 1.

The work of the exegete involves inquiry about the content of a text (what is said) and the context of what has been said (why it is said). Questions about content cover four major areas, namely, textual criticism (the quest for the original wording of a text), lexical data (the meaning of words), grammatical data (the language of the text or the relationship of words to one another), and historical-cultural background (the relationship of words and ideas to the background and culture of the author and the audience). Contextual questions are both historical and literary. Historical context deals with general historical settings of a text.[3] As an example, some historical issues for the book of Colossians include the background of the city of Colossae, its geography, people, religions, economy and political structure. Literary context deals with the reason for saying what has been said and why it was said at a given point in the argument (or narrative) or the specific occasion that led to the writing of the document.[4]

Needless to say, the exegetical task seems to focus more on the "then" of the text than the "now" of contextualized meaning. Nonetheless, an attempt to discover the meaning of a text to its original audience indirectly implies applying that meaning to the contemporary situations with the same impact it had when it was originally written.[5] The original meaning of a text remains non-beneficial to the exegete or a potential consumer unless it is applied to the contemporary world (This is task of application and it is hermeneutical). In this respect, exegesis could be considered as a cross-cultural exercise in which the exegete negotiates between the biblical context and his/her own context by bridging time gap, language gap, cultural gap, socio-economic gap and so on. As a cultural mediator, the exegete may not always have to stick to some hard and fast rules which he/she may consider as a standard. How one mediates between the Bible culture and another culture may be different from how he/she does it for a different culture. The reason is that deriving the meaning of a text for a given society is contextually informed; contexts are different and hence the mediation differs. We shall look at this issue more closely later in the study.

---

[3] Gordon Fee, *New Testament Exegesis: A Handbook for Students and Pastors* (Philadelphia: The Westminster Press, 1983), 25.
[4] Fee, *New Testament Exegesis*, 25.
[5] Victor H. Matthews and James C. Moyer, *The Old Testament: Text and Context* (Grand Rapids, MI: Baker Academic, 2012), 27.

Biblical exegesis has a three-fold dimension; it is an investigation, art and a conversation.[6] It is an investigation about a text, its source, its background, meaning, audience and any other related issue. At the same time, it is an art because it requires the application of some laid down principles and skills. More so, exegesis is a conversation (or communication about texts and their meanings) in that it is done by engaging other people (both living and dead). The accumulated beliefs and practices of the Church are important to the exegete because they help him/her to avoid the mistakes of past scholars and to build upon sound foundations laid in the past. The exegete is expected to listen to others, whether he/she agrees with them or not.

There are various methods of conducting exegetical analysis. Gorman has grouped these approaches into three main categories, namely, synchronic approach (including narrative criticism, social-scientific criticism, rhetorical criticism and socio-rhetorical criticism[7]), diachronic approach (historical-critical method) and existential approach.[8] The synchronic approach engages the final form of the text as we have in the Bible. This approach uses various methods to analyze the text itself and to analyze it in relation to the world in which it first appeared; it deals with the world behind the text. Therefore, issues related to the "prehistory" of the text, including, oral traditions, possible written sources (such as the hypothetical sources called J, E, D, and P in the Pentateuch or Q sources in the Gospels) are not relevant in the synchronic approach.

The diachronic approach, on the other hand, deals with the origin and development of the biblical text. It seeks to discover the situation out of which the text arose and the historical, religious and cultural setting described by the text. Methodologies that fall under this approach include form criticism, source criticism, tradition criticism, historical criticism, and redaction criticism, all of which are higher critical approaches to Biblical Studies. This methodology compares the text with a shell with many layers such that if one could carefully peel away the layers he/she could discover the core and its original context.

The third method is the existential approach which neither analyses the history behind nor the history within the text, but rather engages the text itself and tries to deduce the reality beyond it as testified in it (the text). This method therefore treats the text not as an end in itself but as a means of discovering the reality behind the text. Gorman describes this approach as

---

[6] Michael J. Gorman, *Elements of Biblical Exegesis: A Basic Guide for Students and Ministers*, Revised and Expanded Edition (Grand Rapids, MI: Baker Academic, 2009), 10.
[7] The socio-rhetorical method has gained scholarly attention in recent years and so we will discuss it in greater details later in the study.
[8] Gorman, *Elements of Biblical Exegesis*, 13.

self-involving because "readers do not treat the text as a historical or literary artifact but as something to engage experientially—something that could or should affect lives."[9] Each of these approaches has its advantages and disadvantages but they are all aimed at finding the meaning of the text so that it can be applied in a contemporary situation.

The question of the role of the Holy Spirit in biblical exegesis is an important one that often arises in discussions. Some people are of the view that no sound biblical exegesis can be done without insight from the Holy Spirit. As the author and interpreter of Scripture the Holy Spirit is the only person (together with the Father and Son) who has the true understanding of Scripture. Paul alludes to this point when he says the Holy Spirit is the only one who understands the things of God (1 Cor. 2:11). Therefore, only those who have the Spirit (that is genuine Christians) can interpret (understand and apply) God's word correctly. If so then the exegete must be a spiritual person, always relying on the Spirit to communicate meaning to him/her. Opposing this view vehemently are those who argue that the Bible is like any other book which has to be interpreted based on the applicable rules applying to the various genres that have been chosen to write it. In this regard, the argument proceeds, one's faith or lack of it has nothing to do with finding meaning in the text of the Bible. Of course this reasoning does not rely on the contents of the Bible for support. Rather, it relies on rules of language use. We think that is possible for a non-believer to understand the Bible because an unbeliever can follow effectively the rules of interpretation.

The role of the Holy Spirit in the exegetical process does not take away the need to study and apply tested principles of biblical interpretation. Language is used in writing and one cannot understand the written text without engaging the rules of the Language and the writing style used. Paul makes this point when he instructed Timothy, "Study [be diligent] to show yourself approved unto God, a workman that needs not to be ashamed, rightly dividing the word of truth" (2 Tim. 2:15). Paul is pointing out the need to work toward acquiring the knowledge required to interpret Scripture correctly. This means that there is nothing wrong with learning how to interpret Scripture correctly as an academic discipline. This point is important because we hear people say that academic work has nothing to do with biblical interpretation; the Holy Spirit will teach people how to read Scripture without any academic exercise. Experience teaches that people, who refuse to learn basic rules of interpretation, claiming that the Holy Spirit will "drop" interpretation into the minds, usually end up giving wrong interpretations. The reason is that the

---

[9] Gorman, *Elements of Biblical Exegesis*, 18.

help of the Holy Spirit is not a substitute for what God expects us to use our mental faculties to acquire. God created us in his own image by giving us the ability to think and acquire wisdom from him. Indeed, the Holy Spirit helps people as they study to interpret Scripture.

Conclusion

The aim of any serious Christian is to know the will of God and to live in accordance with it. God's will for our lives is in the Scriptures, and as such, all serious Christians must be involved in biblical exegesis at one level or the other in order to understand and live in accordance with the will of God. We do exegesis in order to arrive at the meaning of a Bible text. We can use the synchronic, diachronic and existential approaches to do exegesis. Despite the different approaches, exegesis is an investigation, art and communication. Having introduced the study in this chapter we now proceed to engage closely the issues raised.

Review Exercise

1. Explain the term exegesis. How different is exegesis from hermeneutics?

2. Explain each of the three major approaches to exegesis outlined in this chapter. How will you differentiate between them?

3. Has the Holy Spirit any role to play in biblical exegesis? Explain your answer.

4. To what extent is exegesis a science, dialogue or art?

5. Critically examine the role of the exegete in the Christian community.

6. Critique the assertion that "The Holy Spirit is the true interpreter of Scripture who will teach us all truth; therefore, there is no need for studying exegetical principles."

Chapter 2

Textual Analysis

Biblical exegesis involves two stages, namely, analysis and synthesis. The first stage comprises analyses related to textual, contextual, grammatical and literary dimensions of the text. It informs the exegete's understanding of the passage and lays the appropriate foundation on which the second stage, synthesis, is built. In the second stage, the exegete brings together the various findings about the text from the textual, contextual, grammatical, and literary analyses conducted in the first stage. What goes into the different tasks involved in each of these stages? How are these tasks conducted? The present and other chapters that follow attempt to answer these questions.

What is Textual Analysis?

Textual analysis (criticism) refers to the process of arriving at the original text. It involves the comparison of all known manuscripts of a given text in order to trace the history of variations within them so as to discover the original form of a text. This step is crucial because both the meaning and applications derived from the text will be useless if it is found that they were derived from a wrong text. If so, then the foremost task is to be sure that the text the exegete is dealing with is a reliable Hebrew or Greek manuscript. Textual criticism is both an art and science in that it involves the collection and comparison of data as well as the application of certain rules in determining what the original wording of a text is.

What factors necessitate textual analysis? Here are some of the reasons why biblical exegetes have to conduct textual analysis.[1] Firstly, none of the original autographs exists currently. What has survived till today are only copies of the original texts. Scholars have to determine the original wording by studying the various ancient manuscripts of biblical texts that have survived till today.

Secondly, various copies of surviving ancient manuscripts differ in their actual wording due to scribal errors that crept in through the process of copying and re-copying.[2] The differences in wording exhibited by available copies make it

---

[1] Gleaned from www.theopedia.com/Biblical criticism (Accessed on July 21, 2018).
[2] In our world, we can produce the exact copy of text by photocopying, or reprinting. The ancient world relied on hand-copying to produce copies of texts.

necessary to determine what the original author wrote. The different copies of the biblical text lead to different readings of the same passage which we refer to as **textual variants** or **variant readings**. Textual variants may involve "changes in a letter, a word, a phrase or even additions and omissions of whole sentences or paragraphs."[3] In other words, textual variants are variations in characters, words, sentences or paragraphs that occur between different manuscripts of the same text. New Testament (NT) scholars agree that the longer ending of Mark's Gospel (16:9-20) and the account of the woman caught in adultery (John 7:53-8:11), for instance, constitute textual variants (up to a paragraph or more). Major New Testament textual variants include the following.

(1). **Textus Receptus** (Latin, meaning "received text") refers to the succession of printed Greek texts of the New Testament which was first put together by Desiderius Erasmus in the 16th century. It was the base text for English translations like William Tyndale's version and King James Version (KJV). While we regard the KJV as a reliable translation, and certainly adequate for learning God's truth, we need to state that numerous additional ancient resources have gone into constructing the more modern Greek texts which were not available to the translators of the KJV. Wayne Jackson notes the following points which lead him to conclude that the KJV should not in any way be considered superior to any of the modern translations.[4]

    i.   Thousands of manuscripts (substantial or in fragments), much older than those employed by the KJV translators have been discovered and incorporated into modern texts.

    ii.   Ancient versions (early translations of the Hebrew/Aramaic and Greek texts), not used by the KJV translators, have been referenced for the latest Greek texts.

    iii.   Thousands of comparative Patristic (early post-apostolic writers) quotations (containing virtually the whole of the New Testament record) have added tremendously to the knowledge of the restoration of a reliable text.

    iv.   Significant advances have been made in the study of the Hebrew, Aramaic, and Greek languages during the past two hundred years.

---

[3] Craig L. Blomberg and Jennifer Foutz Markley, *A Handbook of New Testament Exegesis* (Grand Rapids, MI: Baker Academic, 2010), 5.
[4] Wayne Jackson, "What About the Textus Receptus"? https://www.christiancourier.com/articles/619-what-about-the-textus-receptus (Accessed on 5th February, 2019).

(2). **The Majority Text or Byzantine text-type** (also called Traditional Text, Ecclesiastical Text, Constantinopolitan Text, Antiocheian Text, or Syrian Text) refers to a large group of manuscripts with striking similarities and which constitute the majority of all known manuscripts. The striking similarities among these manuscripts set them apart from other manuscripts. They are however not older manuscripts. These are primarily later manuscripts found in the regions of the Byzantine Empire (the eastern remnant of the Roman Empire that lasted through the Middle Ages). It is for this reason that these manuscripts are usually called the Byzantine Text form (or Text Type).

(3). The modern critical texts (for instance, *Novum Testamentum Graece*) are based on the oldest manuscripts and versions (from the 100's to the 600's). They agree with one another much more than any of them agree with the Received Text or the Majority Text. Most modern English translations of the New Testament including, the American Standard Version, New International Version, Revised Standard version, New Revised Standard Version, New American Standard Version, English Standard Version, Jerusalem Bible and New American Bible are based on it.

Thirdly, many of the available manuscripts contain incomplete sections of the original. It is difficult but very necessary to put the pieces together to reconstruct the biblical text. Textual criticism therefore involves a reconstruction of the biblical texts based usually on incomplete sections available today. This means that in the process one section may complement another section and so on.

Fourthly, thousands of extant manuscripts (of varying textual content) dating from the 3rd century to the 16th century are available for consideration in textual criticism.[5] The existence of many different manuscripts necessitates textual analysis, because without this process we would not know which of the many extant manuscripts to use for our study. However, having many manuscripts of the biblical text is both a fortune and misfortune for the exegete. It is a fortune because with such an abundance of material the exegete can be reasonably certain that the original text is to be found somewhere in it. However, the abundance of material is likewise a problem to the exegete, because (as noted earlier) no two copies are exactly alike and the number of variants keeps increasing as more copies become available. This is especially so in the light of the ideal that each piece of evidence must be used in order to identify the original by detecting possible corruption of the New Testament text.

---

[5] There are over five thousand (5000) copies of the NT that have survived till date.

Fifthly, manuscript evidence suggests different textual traditions that developed geographically over time, and it is through textual criticism that this situation can be handled effectively. That is to say, although it is true that no two manuscripts are identical, it is also equally true that many are so much alike that they tend to group themselves into major families of texts. Each group or family, exhibiting certain distinguishing features, is called **a text type**. Copies belonging to the same text type usually emerge from a particular geographical area and are based on a parent copy that originated from that area. New Testament text types emerged in the early centuries of the church from three major regions, namely, the West, Alexandria and Byzantine. Major Old Testament text types include Masoretic Text (including, Aleppo Codex, Leningrad Codex, Dead Sea Scrolls) and Septuagint (including, Codex Vaticanus, Codex Sinaiticus, Dead Sea Scrolls). The exegete can learn enough about this from scholarly articles and commentaries and make his/her own textual decisions. Textual information in the footnotes of scholarly translations is very helpful in this regard. It is the work of textual analysts which brought this fact to bear.

New Testament textual critics rely basically on three main sources to reconstruct the New Testament text: (1) Greek manuscripts such as papyri, majuscules (or uncials), and minuscules; (2) ancient translations such as Latin (esp. the Vulgate), Syriac, Coptic, Ethiopic, Georgian, Slavonic, Armenian, etc.); and (3) patristic citations (such as from the works of Church Fathers like Justin Martyr, Irenaeus, Clement of Alexandria, Origen, Athanasius, Eusebius, Cyril of Alexandria).[6]

For Old Testament criticism, there are usually two to four sources to consider:[7]

1. A "Majority Text" — the Hebrew tradition of the Masoretic Text (MT), found primarily in late manuscripts but universal in those late manuscripts.

2. The Old Greek [or the Septuagint] —a version, but made at a relatively early date, from materials clearly distinct from the MT, and surviving in manuscripts earlier than the oldest copies of the MT.

---

[6] Blomberg and Markley, *A Handbook of New Testament Exegesis*, 2-4.
[7] Robert B. Waltz, *The Encyclopedia of New Testament Textual Criticism* (NP:NP, Ny), 717.

3. A handful of Hebrew fragments (e.g. the Dead Sea Scrolls and the Genizah fragments), some of which agree with MT, some with the Old Greek, and some with neither.

4. For the Pentateuch, we also have the Samaritan version.

More often than not, Old Testament textual critics are confronted with only two independent witnesses (namely, MT and Old Greek), and so they decide how to proceed with their work. Old Testament textual critics agree that the MT is the most reliable witness to the original text. The MT is based on direct transmission in the original language and has been transmitted through the various epochs with great care, though it is also not entirely free from textual problems. The LXX is used as the primary text only when the MT is believed to be corrupt in a particular instance. In order of their relative importance to textual criticism, scholars place various Old Testament sources as follows: Dead Sea Scrolls, Samaritan Pentateuch, Septuagint, Aquila, Symmachus, Theodotion, Peshitta, and Targums.

What does Textual Criticism Entail?

Textual criticism entails the comparison of the various readings in order to decide which one is the **preferred reading**. The purpose of textual criticism is to reconstruct as closely as possible the original biblical text. The task is divided into two stages. The first stage focuses on the collection and reconstruction of Hebrew variants, while the second deals with the evaluation of variants to determine which one is "original".[8] The task requires sifting through all available materials, carefully collating and comparing each manuscript with all others in order to detect the errors and changes in the text, and thus to decide which variant reading at any given point is more likely to be original. Through the comparison of manuscripts, textual critics establish the degree of certainty of each text or passage. The degree of certainty established for a particular text by a translation team (for a particular version of the Bible) informs their decisions as to whether a particular verse(s) should be included in the main text or footnote (with some comments clarifying the decision taken) or be omitted altogether. This may be the reason for which a particular verse may be missing or footnoted in a given version of the Bible.

---

[8] Emmanuel Tov, *Textual Criticism of the Hebrew Bible* (Minneapolis: Fortress Press, 2001), np. Pdf

Guidelines for Deciding which Reading is "Original"

Textual criticism is guided by a number of rules, some of which we outline below.[9]

i. **The older version is preferable.** The older version is usually closer to the era in which the original was written and so would not have suffered so much from distortions that occurs during the transmission of texts from generation to generation. This means that if manuscripts A and B of the same text, date 233 CE and 321 CE respectively, A must be given priority over B because it (A) is closer to the date the original was written than B. Yet, there is the need for discernment as some older versions may contain corrupted words and some later manuscripts may contain more reliable readings.

ii. **The reading with the widest geographical acceptance is preferable.** A reading that appears in many text types and over a wide geographical area is more likely to be original than one that occurs only in a few text types and over a narrow geographical area. For example, a text that is attested by different text types from Rome, Asia, and North Africa is more likely to be original than one that is found only in Rome.

iii. **The reading which emerges from the more accurately preserved textual traditions is preferable.** Textual critics have identified some textual traditions to be more prone to making "mistakes, harmonisations, and secondary additions." With this in mind, text types that emerge from textual traditions identified as more accurate should be preferred.

iv. **The more difficult and more obscure reading is preferable.** Scribes tend to make texts smoother and easier to read rather than making them rough and difficult to read. To achieve this, scribes change words, insert some words for explanation and do other things. In most cases therefore, textual critics should assume the more difficult reading as the original. This principle may not always be true though.

---

[9] We have gleaned most of the ideas from Blomberg and Markley, *A Handbook of New Testament Exegesis*, 19-24.

Textual Analysis

v. **The shorter reading is preferable.** Scribes found it very difficult to delete God's word. They however, sometimes decided to add certain things to clarify some points to the readers. In rare cases scribes omitted some words in order to smoothen texts. As a general rule therefore, the exegete must prefer the shortest reading as original except when "context and other variants indicate that a shorter reading has occurred" in an attempt by the scribe to smoothen the text by omitting certain portions.

vi. **The reading that most closely fits the style and diction of the author is preferable.** When in doubt, evaluate the text in question against the rest of the book to ascertain if it fits the style and diction of the author as exhibited in that book or another book by the same author.

vii. **The reading that reflects the author's context and theological framework is preferable.** An author usually gives consistent theology in his writings. The exegete can determine which portion is to be taken as original by determining whether the portion in doubt is theologically consistent with the rest of the book or not. A different theology points to the work of scribes.

viii. **When variants exist in parallel passages, assume the less-harmonious one as original.** Studies have shown that the scribes were more interested in harmonizing seeming contradictions in parallel passages than introducing new problems into the texts. The exegete must take a decision that allows the various authors to express themselves in their own style.

How to Determine the Limits of a Text

A passage chosen for exegesis must be a self-contained unit. If you have been given a specific group of verses this step might not be necessary, but if not, you need to determine where a given text begins and ends. Determining where the unit begins and ends may be difficult for new exegetes. Below are some clues the reader can use to determine specific sections/units of texts.[10]

---

[10] The clues have been taken from Walther C. Kaiser Jr., *Toward an Exegetical Theology: Biblical Exegesis for Preaching and Teaching* (Grand Rapids, Michigan: Baker Book House, 1981), 72. We have slightly modified them for our purpose.

i. Themes may offer the reader clues about the book structure by dividing the book into sections. A repeated word, phrase, clause or sentence may act as sectional heading (themes) to begin each part or to close a section. The phrase "the generations of …" appears several times in Genesis as sectional heading. For example, "the generations of the heavens and earth" (Gen. 2:4), "the generations of Adam" (Gen. 5:1), "the generations of Noah" (Gen. 6:9), "the generations of the sons of Noah" (Gen. 10:1), "the generations of Terah" (Gen. 11:27). In Amos 4, the end of a divine judgement is marked by the sad refrain, "Yet you did not return to me, says the Lord" (vss. 6, 8, 9, 10, 11). Amos has another transitional statement "woe to you" (5:18; 6:1, 4). Moreover, five visions conclude the book of Amos, four of them introduced by, "the Lord showed me" (7:1, 4, 7; 8:1). Paul uses the expression "Now concerning …" to introduce most themes in 1 Cor. (7:1, 25; 8:1; 12:1; 16:1).

ii. Transitional conjunctions or adverbs such as then, yet, meanwhile, even though, nonetheless and so on may indicate the beginning of a new section.

iii. A rhetorical question may be used to introduce a new section. For example, "What shall we say then? Shall we sin that grace may increase?" (Rom. 6:1).

iv. Most narratives use change in time, location or setting to introduce new themes and sections. For example, the expression "During the reign of David…" (2 Sam. 21:1) shows the introduction of a new theme.

v. Most epistolary literature uses a vocative voice to shift focus from one group to another and to introduce new themes.

vi. A change in tense, mood, voice or aspect of verb may indicate the introduction of a new section.

vii. Structural features such as chiasm, *inclusio*, alternation and contrast usually mark the end or beginning of a unit.

Translating the Text

Part of the exegete's textual task is to provide a provisional translation of the text based on the source text (Hebrew, Greek or Aramaic). The translation should be accurate, natural and clear. The exegete's knowledge of the biblical languages (Hebrew, Greek and Aramaic) will enhance this step. An exegete who has no working knowledge of the source languages and therefore cannot produce his/her own translation may take alternative translations from few existing translations, preferably from more literal translations like the New Revised Standard Version, New American Standard Version, or English Standard Version. The translation given at this stage may be revised at a later stage of the exegetical process.

Conclusion

Among other things, this chapter has shown that textual analysis is a key step in biblical exegesis. It is very crucial for the exegete to use all available resources to determine the originality of the text he/she is dealing with. Without this step the exegete may finish before realizing that it was the wrong text he/she dealt with. After establishing the limits and authenticity of the text, the exegete provides a provisional translation to work with. This stage is just the beginning of the exegetical process; there are other crucial steps to take. We now proceed to examine some of these other steps.

Review Exercise

1. What is textual criticism? Is textual criticism necessary at all? Explain your answer.

2. How can an exegete determine the originality of a given text?

3. Provide your own English translation of the following passages based on the Hebrew or Greek manuscript.

    a. Gen. 1:26-27

    b. 1 Kings 10:1-5

    c. Ps. 1:1-2

    d. John 1:1

4. What is your response to the assertion that, "The NIV is corrupt because it omits certain verses in the New Testament (eg. Matt. 23:14, Mark 9:44, Mark 9:46, and Mark 11:26)."

5. With examples from Romans show how the flow-of-thought of a biblical writer can be determined.

6. Translate the following passages into your native language.

    a. Heb. 1:1-4

    b. Col. 1:15-20

    c. Col. 2:16-17

Chapter 3

Contextual Analysis

After establishing the best possible original text and providing a working translation of the text, the next thing to do is to consider the context of the text. As noted earlier, exegetical study includes all aspects relevant to the historical and literary contexts of the book from which the passage under consideration is taken. Contextual analysis includes historical context, social context, literary and rhetorical context, among others. This chapter discusses each of these aspects of contextual analysis.

Historical Context

Historical context forms the backdrop for the biblical story. It has to do with a diachronic study of general history behind a given text. It focuses on issues of authorship, date of composition, audience (recipients), occasion and purpose, the socio-economic, political and religious contexts of the book. Additional issues include where the book falls in the life of the author, the circumstances of the author at the time of writing, and the relationship between the author and the recipients. The historical study may engage several areas of biblical backgrounds including, chronology, geography, archeology, culture, literature, society and political institutions.

Information about historical context may be deduced from the biblical books themselves. For example, the author and audience of the book of James may be deduced from the book itself as James and the twelve tribes scattered among the nations (1:1) respectively. In the letter to the church of Philippi, we know from the book itself that Paul was in prison (1:7, 13), he had thought one time that he was getting to the end of his ministry (1:22-23, 2:17), but God encouraged him that he had more to do (1:24-25). In that situation, Paul still had joy from his relationship with the Philippians (1:3-11; 4:10) who had shown concern for him by sending Epaphroditus to him in prison (2:25-30). They had recently sent some gifts to Paul for which reason he thanked them (4:10-20). Paul also indicates that he had heard about some false Jewish teachers who had troubled the church (3:2-6). These data gleaned from the book serves as a guide to the reader in understanding the tone, themes and arguments in the letter.

In the case of a gospel text, the exegete needs to examine two separate but related historical contexts, namely, the historical setting of Jesus (which encompasses the study of the cultural and religious contexts of the first century Palestinian Judaism in which Jesus lived and ministered) and the historical setting, the author and recipients of the passage under consideration, that is, the existential issues that necessitated the writing of the passage. When and where an action takes place in a Bible text must inform the interpretation of the text. For example, the healing of the paralytic in the synagogue where Scripture was being studied on the Sabbath (Mark 3:1-6) has a different impact than healing of the woman with the blood issue (Mark 5:25–34 cf. Matt. 9:20–22, Luke 8:43–48).

Social Context

Social context (world) deals with the history of the world that existed at the same time as the text (it is synchronic, within time). There are different dimensions of the social world of a text. We outline each of these briefly below. One level of social context is the world context, which refers to the information and experience common to humanity in general. For example, the metaphor of light and darkness has universal applicability because it works cross-culturally; it is known in various cultures. All manner of people regard light as that which is required to direct our path (Ps. 119:105) and darkness as confusing our path. More so, the meaning of expressions such as denarius (Matt. 20:2), or a Sabbath day's journey (Acts 1:12) or "high places" (Eph.1:3) were known to both biblical writers and their audiences. The 21st century exegete must understand what they meant in the biblical world in order to make meaning of the texts containing them.

Another aspect of social context is cultural context which refers to the ways of understanding issues pertaining to how people live(d) in a particular society. Most of the data under this level will be strange to our context because we live in a world which is quite different from the world of biblical times. Knowledge of this context is crucial to understanding the text. Included in the cultural context are the society's political, social and religious beliefs and practices, economics, music, art, values, military/war customs, material customs/culture and others. The exegete must deal adequately with any direct mention of, or allusion to any of these areas. The interpreter seeks information regarding the socio-cultural environment that shaped the writing and meaning of the text. For example, the practice of levirate marriage in the Ancient Near East (especially as practiced among ancient Israelites) has to be understood in order to understand Genesis 38. Another example is that Jesus' prohibition of accumulation of earthly treasures (Matt. 6:19) could better be understood if it is studied in the light of the socio-economic situation of his time.

A third aspect of social context is audience context. It deals with the experiences and specific knowledge common to the biblical audience. Such

Contextual Analysis

issues may be tied to a particular era and/or particular community. For example, the people of Jesus' time would understand better first or second-century Roman rule than us. This point helps us to appreciate the disciples' question about when the kingdom will be given to Israel (Acts 1:6). This question was asked because the Jews of Jesus' time were under oppressive Roman rule and hence, were eager to have someone lead them to gain political independence. A misunderstanding of this context will lead to faulty exegesis and wrong application of the text.

The last level of social context is the dynamic context which deals with the relationship that evolves through interactions between the author of a text and the intended audience. Most epistles in the New Testament exhibit this kind of context. They betray an ongoing conversation between the author and the intended audience. Interactions between the author and his audience lead to the evolution of certain contextual factors that become common to the two parties (author and audience). The author then assumes the factors when writing to them. For instance, Paul's first letter to the Corinthians assumes much-shared context because Paul had a long interaction with the Corinthian church before writing his letter to them (for example his baptism of Crispus and household 1:14-16). Also, Paul's greetings in Romans 16:1-15 points to his familiarity with his audience.

Like the historical context, the social world of a biblical book may be obtained by a careful reading of the book itself. For example, the socio-economic context of the book of Amos can be deduced from the book as follows: In those days "commerce thrived (8:5), an upper class emerged (4:1-3), and expensive homes were built (3:15; 5:11; 6:4, 11). The rich enjoyed an indolent, indulgent lifestyle (6:1-6), while the poor became targets for legal and economic exploitation (2:6-7; 5:7, 10-13; 6:12; 8:4-6). Slavery for debt was easily accepted (2:6; 8:6)."[1] The religious context of the same book can also be deduced as follows: Standards of morality had sunk to a low ebb (2:7), shrines provided spiritual identity to the nation (5:5; 8:1-14), people were very religious as evidenced in the many sacrifices they made (4:4), including, peace-offerings (5:22), meal offerings (5:22), thanks offerings (4:5), freewill offerings and tithes (4:4-5). In the book of Isaiah, the phrase "in the year that King Uzziah died" (Is. 6:1) sets the stage for Isaiah's call into ministry.[2] It has nothing to do with the claim that someone prominent must die for your

---

[1] Donald R. Sunukjian, "Commentary on Amos" in *The Bible Knowledge Commentary* (Colorado: David C. Cook, 1983), 1425.
[2] Remember also that this same expression indicates the introduction of a new theme by the writer.

blessing to come to you. Also, the author of Ezra indicates that the events he narrates took place during the Persian rule (Ezra 1:1; 4:6) after the Babylonian captivity (2:1). The writer is giving a clue about the political context within which the events he narrates took place. He does this to help share meaning with the reader. Such information serves as contextual help to the interpreter.

The above examples tell us that background issues may be discovered from the book itself. That notwithstanding, in many cases the information provided by the biblical writer alone is inadequate for a thorough study. One may have to consult secondary sources such as Bible dictionaries, Old Testament and New Testament introductions and commentaries for additional data. Resources such as Bible Dictionaries, Bible Encyclopedia, Bible commentaries will help the exegete obtain reliable historical background of Bible characters and geography. Primary Jewish sources such as the works of Josephus, Philo, The Dead Sea Scrolls[3] and deuterocanonical books[4] are also valuable in this regard.

Literary Context

Literary context has to do with the literary material that surrounds a text. Literary contextual analysis is based on the fact that every word is part of a sentence; every sentence is part of a paragraph; every paragraph is part of a book; and every book is part of the whole of Scripture. From this perspective, every text may be regarded as the center of a series of concentric circles, each of which represents respectively, the immediate context, the larger context, the book context, and the canonical context.[5] Scholars have identified three dimensions of literary context, namely, immediate context, book context and canonical context.

---

[3] English versions of these documents include: *Flavius Josephus, The Complete Works* translated by William Whiston (Nashville: Thomas Nelson Inc., 1998); *The Works of Philo Complete Unabridged*, trans. C.D. Young, updated ed. (Peabody, MA: Hendrickson, 1993); *The Dead Sea Scrolls Today*, rev. ed. (Grand Rapids, MI: Eerdmans, 2010)

[4] These are books which are contained in the Catholic Bible but not in the Protestant Bible. There are seven of such books including Tobit, Judith, 1 & 2 Maccabees, Wisdom of Solomon, Wisdom of Sirach (also called Ecclesiasticus) and Baruch including the Letter of Jeremiah. Each of them belongs to the Catholic Old Testament. By referring to these books as helpful sources of obtaining background information for the study of a biblical book, we (from the Protestant tradition) are in no way endorsing these books as part of the inspired books. We consider them as sources of useful historical information. The Roman Catholics themselves regard these books as belonging to a second canon (Deuterocanon).

[5] Gorman, *Elements of Biblical Exegesis*, 75 and J. Scott Duvall and J. Daniel Hays, *Grasping God's Word*, 2d ed. (Grand Rapids: Zondervan, 2005), 122.

The immediate context of a text includes the text that comes immediately before or after it. In other words, it is the surrounding paragraphs of a verse or the literary material that immediately precedes and that which follows a text. For instance, the immediate context of the story of Nicodemus in John 3 includes John 2 and 4. Also, the immediate context of Deuteronomy 15:1-11 includes 14:22-29 which talks about laws on tithing and 15:12-18 which outlines the law on the release of slaves. The immediate context has the greatest influence on the meaning of a text. As such, the accuracy of the results of the exegetical process depends largely on the exegete's knowledge about it (the immediate context). For this reason, no attempt should be made at explaining the meaning of a text in a broader context without first determining its meaning in the immediate context. The exegete must try to determine the subject of the paragraph or two immediately preceding the text under consideration and also to establish the link between them (if any). The theme (the dominant idea or topic sentence) and structure of the text must be of importance to the exegete as he/she goes through it. Text structure is the pattern of organization within a passage or the way terms are related and interrelated in order to communicate ideas according to mental, linguistic, and literary patterns.[6]

Book context refers to the book in which a passage is located. The entire book must be studied in order to determine its overall purpose and how the text under consideration links up with the other parts of the book. Understanding a writer's general purpose will provide a larger context for each specific passage, and this becomes a tool for discovering the author's original meaning. The exegete may ask the following questions in relation to the book context:

i. Where does this passage occur in the structure of the book?

ii. How does this passage flow from a larger passage or book?

iii. Why was this particular book written?

iv. Of what major section is it a part?

v. What significance does this position have?

vi. What has "happened" (whether in narrative, argument, etc.) in the book so far, and what will happen later?

---

[6] Robert A. Traina, *Methodical Bible Study* (Grand Rapids, Mi: Zondervan, 1985), 36. https://books.google.com.gh/books?id=iahqfr9_uGMC&pg=PA38&lpg=PA38&dq

vii. What appears to be the text's function in the section and in the book as a whole?

viii. How does this passage appear to serve the agenda of the entire work?[7]

It is not always easy to determine an author's overall purpose in a book. Kaiser suggests four ways by which this can be achieved; we present them below.[8]

i. The author may write his purpose in the preface, conclusion or the body of the text. For example, the writer of Luke identifies his purpose in the first four verses.

ii. The parenetical sections of New Testament epistles may carry some applications that the author himself has made of the factual and doctrinal portions of the text. The exhortation of the author may give clue of his purpose.

iii. In the case of biblical narrative or story, the content and the arrangement of the entire book or passage may also give a clue about the author's purpose. For example, one can deduce that the purpose of Genesis 1 is to make the point that God created the universe and whatever it contains.

iv. In the absence of any clear clue the exegete must determine the purpose by studying the various topic sentences and themes. The connection between them is used to work out the purpose.

The last aspect of literary context is canonical context, referring to the relationship between a text and the rest of Scripture. The exegete should keep in mind the diversity of the biblical text. The canonical context reminds us that the Bible was revealed progressively and so as more revelations were received things became clearer than before. Therefore, it is not appropriate to base one's doctrine on only the early part of the Bible without taking into consideration the other (or later) parts. For example, a doctrine of the Holy Spirit based on Genesis 1 alone will fall short of what the Bible reveals about the Holy Spirit in the later portions. Similarly, the doctrine of Trinity cannot be

---

[7] With the exception of questions 2 & 3, all questions were adapted from Gorman, *Elements of Biblical Exegesis*, 76.
[8] Kaiser Jr., *Toward an Exegetical Theology*, 79.

formulated based on the teachings of the Old Testament alone; New Testament teachings must be considered as well.

The seeming contradictions we sometimes encounter when we seek to find the meaning of Bible texts can be dealt with if we take this point seriously. Failure to consider all Scripture concerning an issue may lead to obscurity in understanding and perception of certain texts as contradicting each other. In our view, "contradictions" between two parts of Scripture appear when: (1) we have not interpreted one of the passages correctly or (2) we have not interpreted both passages rightly. The way to go about it is to check the validity of the interpretation of both of them based not only on the immediate and book contexts but also based on the entire Bible. For example, Paul's and James's comments on faith and justification (Rom. 3:28 cf. James 2:24) may seem contradictory. However, a careful reading of the two writers in their own contexts resolves the tension.[9]

Conclusion

The relevance of contextual analyses in exegesis has been established in this chapter. An interpretation done without considering context is bound to be wrong. Therefore, the exegete must take contextual issues seriously and deal with all necessary aspects of it before attempting to interpret a text. Apart from textual and contextual analyses, the exegete also needs to deal with grammatical issues. The next chapter takes care of grammatical analysis.

Review Exercise

1. Why is immediate context so crucial in biblical exegesis?

2. Deduce the historical background of Philemon based on the content of the book. How does the author develop his message?

3. What social context can you deduce from Paul's letter to the Colossian church?

4. Conduct a background study of the book of Jonah. In what ways should this background study affect the way we interpret the book of Jonah?

---

[9] For further clarification on this matter consult, Frederick Mawusi Amevenku and Isaac Boaheng, "Reconciling saving faith and works of the law in Paul and James" in *Ghana Journal of Religion and Theology* Vol. 7 (1) 2017: 66-80.

5. What social context can you derive from the book of Joel? How similar or different is this context from your context? What lessons can be learnt for the interpretation of the book?

6. Does Paul contradict James on faith and works? Explain your answer based on the situation each author addresses.

7. What possible socio-economic situation informs Jesus' teachings in Matthew 6:19-24?

Chapter 4

Grammatical Analysis

Grammatical analysis involves four main tasks, namely, lexicology (the meaning of words), morphology (the form of words), grammatical function of words (parts of speech), and syntax (the relationships of words). Not all grammatical units may be examined because not all of them may have the same value in determining the message of a specific biblical text. What the exegete needs to do at this stage is to examine theologically significant words and phrases to discover their significance in the text (lexical analysis). That is to say, the exegete must focus especially on those words and phrases that may be pertinent to the specific issue under consideration or on what he/she feels is not obvious to his/her readers and what makes a genuine difference in the meaning of the passage. What does each aspect of grammatical analysis entail? We attend to this and other questions in this chapter.

Word Study

A word refers to a verbal symbol (either written or spoken) used in reference to a concept. In dealing with words, the exegete aims at understanding the concept conveyed in the host language and deciding the appropriate word that will evoke as similar a concept as possible in the receptor language. Said differently, the purpose of word study is to determine the meaning of a word as intended by the author and to decide how to convey this meaning to the exegete's target world. Tools for conducting a word study include lexica, theological dictionaries and concordances.

There are no hard and fast rules regarding how one can go about this important exercise. We however, agree with Kaiser that the task can be handled using the following guiding principles.[1] Firstly, the intended meaning of a word is informed by the custom of the author and the general usage at the times that he wrote them. Like authors of today, biblical authors do not usually explain words whose meanings are familiar to them and their audience. The recipients understand the writer because they assume the common meaning. When unfamiliar words are used, they are explained. For example, the Aramaic word *Rabuni* (Heb. *Rabbi*) is explained as a teacher

---

[1] Gleaned from Kaiser, *Toward an Exegetical Theology*, 106-108.

(John 1:38) in order to help non-Aramaic readers to understand it. How the original audience understood a word or how it is explained in the text is what matters and not the root meaning of the word. Therefore, the exegete must avoid giving more interpretative weight to the etymology of words than is necessary. It is not always that words carry the meaning of their roots. Secondly, the meaning of a word or expression can also be determined from the usage of that same word or expression by the same author either in the same writing or in a different one. For example, Paul's use of the phrase "works of law" Romans 3:20; Galatians 2:16 [three times]; 3:2, 5, 10 may throw light on how we are to understand this expression in Romans 3:28.

Thirdly, the meaning of a word may also be obtained from an appositional phrase used by the author or from an editorial comment by the author. For example, the meaning of the word temple in John 2:19 can be determined from verse 21 as Christ's body. The grammatical unit to which a word belongs also gives clues about its meaning. For example, the word "man" may be used as a noun or verb and the meaning changes depending on how it is used. Fourthly, contextual antithesis and contrasts can also give clues about the meaning of words. For example, Paul's contrast between those who live "according to flesh" with those who live "according to the Spirit" (Rom. 8:5-8), gives a clue regarding his usage of "flesh" and "Spirit." Fifthly, Hebrew poetry uses parallelism to give clues to word meaning. In some cases (especially the Gospels), word meaning can also be determined by studying parallel passages, either in the same book or in another book. The use of synonymous words (synonymous parallelism) or antithetic words (antithetical parallelism) is the key. For instance, in Colossians 2:17 the word "shadow" and "reality" (NIV) are contrasted; Psalm 5:1, 2 uses parallelism in which the expression "Listen to" (v. 2) throws light on "Give ear" (v. 1, NIV).

Guidelines for Word Study

The following guidelines are very helpful in conducting an effective word study.[2]

i. Most words have a range of meanings, so that one word does double duty with regard to the concept of symbols. Word meanings can overlap with the meanings of other words.

ii. Word meanings change over time; therefore, it is the context rather than the original meaning of the term that must

---

[2] These guidelines have been adapted from Blomberg and Markley, *A Handbook of New Testament Exegesis*, 119.

	determine how the exegete will appropriately define and understand any given word.
iii.	In addition to having denotative meaning (literal meaning of a word), words also have connotative value (that is, special meaning for a particular person or group, perhaps only in certain contexts), which is why it is important to survey the literary and historical backgrounds of a passage before studying the words in that passage.
iv.	Individual words function with the rest of the words in the context to express larger sets of concepts; they can rarely accomplish the feat of expressing a complete concept themselves.
v.	The priority in determining word meaning should almost always go to the findings of synchronic (that is, "with time") analysis of the word under study rather than those of diachronic (that is, "through time") analysis.

Morphological Analysis

Morphological analysis has to do with the identification, analysis and description of the structure of a given language's morphemes and other linguistic units, such as root words, affixes, parts of speech, intonations and stresses, or implied context. It refers to the way words are formed or put together (e.g., with something at the beginning of the word— a prefix, or at the end of the word— a suffix, or in the middle). The exegete needs to assess the kind of usage a given case, tense, mood or voice reflects. Issues like the use or omission of article must be looked into.

A case in point is John 1:1 where the omission of the Greek definite article *ho* before *theos* in the expression "*kai theos ēn ho logos*" has generated so much debate. Should the expression be translated as "and the Word was a god" or "and the Word was God"? The Jehovah Witnesses argue for the former while orthodox Christians support the latter. Though a literal translation may result in the former, the immediate context and the broader context do not allow for such translation. The orthodox position is supported by Colwell's rule which states that "definite predicate nouns which follow the verb usually lack the article."[3] Robertson opines that the lack of the article before *theos* gave John the opportunity to distinguish the subject *ho logos*, from the noun *theos* so as to

---

[3] Blomberg and Markley, *A Handbook of New Testament Exegesis*, 159.

describe the personal nature of the Word.⁴ Bruce's comments on this passage are valuable:

> The structure of the third clause in verse 1, *theos en ho logos*, demands the translation "The Word was God." Since *logos* has the article preceding it, it is marked out as the subject. The fact that *theos* is the first word after the conjunction *kai* (and) shows that the main emphasis of the clause lies on it. Had *theos* as well as *logos* been preceded by the article the meaning would have been that the Word was completely identical with God, which is impossible if the Word was also "with God". What is meant is that the Word shared the nature and being of God, or (to use a piece of modern jargon) was an extension of the personality of God.⁵

Part of Speech

Part of speech (grammatical unit or word class) refers to the linguistic categories of words. The English language has nine parts of speech: nouns, pronouns, verbs, adverbs, adjectives, conjunctions, prepositions, interjections, and articles. The exegete needs to identify each word as one of the word classes listed above and determine its function in the sentence. Nouns refer to names of persons, places or items (eg. Paul, Jerusalem). Pronouns stand in place of nouns (eg. it, she, he, them). Each pronoun must have an antecedent, that is, the noun it refers to. If the text under consideration contains a pronoun whose antecedent is not in it, the antecedent must be determined from the preceding text. Verbs are "doing words" or states of being (eg. is, beat, dance). Adverbs modify verbs (eg. very, slowly, badly). Adjectives qualify nouns (eg. red, black, and small). Conjunctions connect words, phrases and clauses (eg. and, but, although). Prepositions introduce nouns, pronouns, noun phrases and noun clauses (eg. in, for, under). Articles make a noun definite or indefinite. The definite article is "the" and the indefinite article is "a" or "an".

Syntax

Syntax refers to the arrangement of words into phrases and of phrases into sentences. The sentence, not the word or phrase, is considered as the primary linguistic unit for expressing meaning. Sentences come together to form larger units of thought called texts segments, which also come together to form

---

[4] A. T. Robertson, *A Grammar of the Greek New Testament in the Light of Historical Research* (Nashville, TN: Broadman Press, 1934), 767.
[5] F. F. Bruce, *The Gospel of John* (Grand Rapids, MI: Wm. B. Eerdmans, 1983), 31.

Grammatical Analysis 29

paragraphs (prose) or stanzas (poetry). The exegete needs to analyze all these units in his/her work. The exegete identifies the basic structures and syntax of each sentence and analyzes the flow of thought in the passage. This step gives the exegete the opportunity to (1) make provisional grammatical decisions about syntactical relationships; (2) visualize the structure of the passage and to recognize structural patterns (such as *inclusio*, contrasts, parallels, chiasm etc.) and (3) provide a tentative outline and flow of the argument. A sentence diagram may be required to break complex sentences into smaller units.

Conclusion

The exegete decides the grammar for everything in the passage. He or she however, discusses only those items where exegetical decision is crucial to the meaning of the passage. Questions to answer include the following: "Are any grammatical points in doubt?" "Could any sentences, clauses, or phrases be read differently if the grammar were construed differently?" Are there genuine ambiguities that make a definite interpretation of some part of the passage impossible? If so, what at least are the possible options? Honest answers to these questions will help clarify the meaning of the text.

Review Exercise

1. To what extent is grammatical analysis important in the process of arriving at the meaning of a text?

2. Explain the term morphology. How relevant is morphological analysis in exegesis?

3. Carefully explain how to conduct an effective word study.

4. What factors determine the meaning of words in a text?

5. Why is it inappropriate to rely so much on etymological meanings when conducting a word study?

6. Write a paper on the topic: Exegesis and theology of Acts 1:8.

7. Does an exegetical study of Ephesians 1:1-4 support or refute the doctrine of election?

8. How does Paul's view on justification according to Rom. 3:28 contradict or complement James' view in James 2:24? Answer this question through an exegetical analysis.

9. To what extent do you agree that "The Christ Event" is the overriding concern in Romans 21-26 and 5:1-21?

Chapter 5

Literary Analysis

The textual, contextual and grammatical analyses, discussed in the previous chapters, apply to all Bible texts. Aside these and other general analyses, there are rules governing the exegesis of each type of literary form (genre). Literary form refers to a distinctive type of text or the category of text according to form(s) and/or content. In other words, literary analysis comprises identifying the general and specific genre of the passage and how it informs the interpretation of the text. Common Old Testament genres include Narrative, Law, Poetry, Prophecy and Wisdom Literature.[1] New Testament genres include Gospels, Acts of the Apostles, Epistles and Revelation. The purpose of this chapter is to equip the exegete with special exegetical principles related to specific genres of Scripture.

Old Testament Narratives

Biblical narratives usually do not directly teach a doctrine.[2] They tell us what happened in history without endorsing the record as examples for everyone to follow or not. For example, the fact that Solomon's polygamous life is narrated in the Bible cannot be interpreted to mean that the Bible endorses polygamy. Other parts of Scripture are needed to settle the issue. For this reason, not every narrative has an individual identifiable moral application. In other words, people's actions in narratives are not necessarily models for our lives. More so, biblical narratives are selective and incomplete. They record

---

[1] The Law includes the books of Leviticus and Deuteronomy. Books classified as history include Genesis, Exodus, Numbers, Joshua, Judges, 1 and 2 Samuel, 1 and 2 Kings, 1 and 2 Chronicles, Ezra, Nehemiah, and Acts. The books of Proverbs, Job and Ecclesiastes are classified as Wisdom Literature. These books are intended to teach about divinity and about virtue. Poetic books include Songs of Solomon, Lamentations and Psalms. Narrative books include the Gospels and the books of Ruth, Esther, and Jonah. There are 21 letters in the NT, from Romans to Jude, referred to as epistles. Old Testament books of Isaiah through Malachi, and the NT book of Revelation belong to prophetic and apocalyptic literature.

[2] We have gleaned this paragraph from Gordon Fee and Douglas Stuart, *How to Read the Bible for all its Worth* 3rd ed. (Grand Rapids, MI: Zondervan Publishing House, 1993), 91-92.

only the relevant portions of events (cf. John 21: 25) that give either explicit or implicit teachings. What we offer here is a brief outline of the principles that must guide exegesis of narratives.

   i.   Determine the general or controlling theme of the text after reading through.

   ii. Follow carefully the plot development and shape of the text. Biblical narratives usually revolve around four key elements, namely: plot, characters, setting and point of view and hence every serious interpreter must look at the text through the lens of each of these elements.[3] The plot for biblical narratives usually unfolds in this pattern: (i) Background (exposition); (ii) Crisis (complication); (iii) Resolution; and (iv) Conclusion (denouement).

   iii. Identify key people, key actions and key terms and theological/cultural concepts.

       a. Pay attention to details, even the small details.
       b. Observe particular information.
       c. Ask questions: Who are the main characters? How does the dialogue help me understand the text?
       d. What needs to be resolved?

   iv. Determine the role played by each character and the lessons that can be learnt from them.

Old Testament Laws

One of the most difficult genres of the Bible is Law. The applicability of the Old Testament laws to the lives of Christians has generated huge arguments.[4] We suggest the following steps when dealing with laws.

---

[3] Steven D. Mathewson, *The Art of Preaching Old Testament Narrative* (Grand Rapid, MI: Baker Academics, 2002), np. https://books.google.com.gh/books?id=xh0HXkcf_TIC&pg=PT4&

[4] For more on Old Testament laws consult Frederick M. Amevenku and Isaac Boaheng, "Analysis of Law and Gospel in God's Salvific Plan" in *ERATS* Vol. 2, No. 1 (February) 2016, 188-212.

1. Determine the category within which the law falls. This rule will help the interpreter in defending God's word against modern social critics. People may say that the Old Testament laws prohibit homosexuality and cooking a young goat in the mother's milk, and therefore cooking a goat in its mother's milk must be condemned just as we condemn homosexuality today. An issue of this nature may be resolved by putting the laws in their categories of ceremonial, moral or civil. In addition, the interpreter must determine whether the law is casuistic (conditional, applying only to a certain group of people under certain circumstances) or apodictic (absolute with universal application).

2. Study any available parallel or anything that Jesus or the apostles said about it.[5]

3. Determine the rationale behind the law. The law that prohibits one gender from wearing the dress of the opposite gender (in Deut. 22:5) was given because in those days people disguised themselves in the dress of their opposite sex and went into the tents of their homosexual partners to have homosexual affairs. God wanted to expose such people.

4. Determine whether or not it is renewed in the New Testament. The interpreter must become aware of how the law has been renewed or modified by Jesus. The theses and antitheses in Matt. 5 is a classic example of Jesus' interpretation of the Old Testament Law.

5. Draw theological and situational analogies between Christians today and the original audience. Points of similarities and points of differences in the culture of the original audience and that of the contemporary audience should serve as the foundation for developing universal principles from the text.

6. Develop universal principles from the text that can be applied to contemporary Christian living. These principles should: (1) be reflected in the text; (2) be timeless; (3) be in agreement with holistic theology of the Bible; (4) not be culturally bound; (5) be consistent with New Testament teaching and (6) be relevant to both old and new believers.

---

[5] This principle worked very well in our example in chapter 8 on the applicability of laws on food to the New Testament believer.

Psalms

There are many different types of Psalms in the Bible and they served many different purposes in ancient Israel. There is a sense in which the Psalms may be regarded as worship poems and songs reflecting a wide range of emotions that the various worshippers expressed. Through the use of the Psalms, worshippers are able to express a wide variety of their emotions to God, whether anger or pain, sorrow or joy, anxiety or excitement, appreciation or disgust. Since the historical context for each Psalm may not be easily determined from the content of the Psalm, it is usually helpful to let the surrounding Psalms in the collection give a clue about the context of the Psalm you seek to interpret.

The following steps are recommended for dealing with the Psalms.

   i. Determine the type of the Psalm. Based on the content of a psalm we may classify them as praise, imprecatory, thanksgiving, lament or a royal, penitential, or messianic psalm.

   ii. Use the type to determine the mood of the speaker.

   iii. The context and the period of composition must be determined.

   iv. Interpret imprecatory psalms in the light of the New Testament. For example, interpret Psalm 35 in the light of Matthew 5:43-45.

Prophecy

We suggest the following exegetical principles for Prophetic Literature.

   1. Interpret as literally as possible.

   2. The interpretation must not contradict any other prophecy elsewhere in the Bible. This principle is taught in 2 Peter 1:20-21. Prophecies must not be interpreted privately, meaning our interpretation must be in harmony with other Scripture texts.

   3. Interpretation of prophecy must be Christo-centric as all prophecies point to Jesus Christ in one way or the other. The fulfillment of Israel's prophetic hope as portrayed in the Old Testament is found in the person and work of Jesus Christ and the Church. For example, the temple of the old covenant was a type or foreshadowing of the glory of Christ. Jesus fulfills the Old Testament feasts.

4. Interpret unfulfilled prophecy in the light of fulfilled prophecy. If the prophecy is predictive determine if fulfilled, unfulfilled, or conditional.

5. Determine whether the prophecy is conditional or unconditional. A conditional prophecy will be fulfilled only if the condition is met. An example of such is Moses' promise to Israel of God's blessings upon the nation pending her obedience (Lev. 26:3-13).

6. For prophetic symbolism and imagery, follow the principles given on symbols, making sure that interpretation of such imagery would be entirely clear as the original author intended.

    i. Note the qualities of the literal object implied by the symbol.

    ii. Try to discover from the context the purpose for using the symbol.

    iii. Use any explanation given in the context to connect the symbol and the truth it teaches. If the symbol is not explained, then use every clue found in the immediate context or in any part of the book where the figure occurs.

    iv. If the symbol which was clear to the initial readers is not clear to modern readers, state explicitly what the barrier is for the modern reader.

    v. Observe the frequency and distribution of a symbol (how often it is used and where it is found), but allow each to control the meaning. Do not force symbols into preconceived schemes of uniformity.[6]

The Gospels

The Gospels are the first four books of the NT, which are Matthew, Mark, Luke and John. The four gospel accounts address four separate communities with different existential concerns such that the aspect of Jesus' life that was needed to address the concerns of one community was different from what was

---

[6] Adapted from A. Berkeley Mickelsen, *Interpreting the Bible* (Grand Rapids, MI: Wm. B. Eerdmans Publishing, 1963), 278.

required in addressing the concerns of another community. The first three gospels present Jesus' ministry from a common standpoint with different perspectives. They are referred to as the Synoptics (or the Synoptic Gospels). The fourth gospel writer was probably aware of what existed in the Synoptics and selected materials to complement what the Synoptics already contained.

The following exegetical guidelines are applicable to the Gospels.

1. Compare the passage under consideration with any parallel accounts in the other Gospels, especially if dealing with the Synoptic Gospels. The Synoptics have many parallel accounts (eg. compare Matt. 5-7 with Luke 6:17-49). In comparing parallel passages, the exegete must not attempt to harmonize these accounts.

2. Study the plot, characters, organization, and major themes of the passage not only to appreciate a given saying or narrative in its present context in the Gospels but also to "understand the nature of the composition of the Gospels as wholes, and thus to interpret any one of the Gospels itself, not just isolated facts about the life of Jesus."[7]

3. For parables, the exegete must carefully consider the main scope and get familiar with its historical-cultural context. There is the need to uncover what event prompted the parable. A parable should not be used as the sole basis for formulating a doctrine. Avoid focusing too much on the details. Study the structure of the parable and determine the main points. Clues to arriving at the main point may be obtained from the prelude to the parable, (Luke 18:9; 19: 11); or an epilogue to the parable (Matt 15:13; Luke 16:9).

Acts of the Apostles

Acts is the only historical book in the New Testament. It deals with the historical "development of the early church after the Ascension of Jesus"[8] and serves as the background for most of the epistles. The epistles cannot fully be appreciated without understanding the book of Acts. The main exegetical

---

[7] Fee and Stuart, *How to Read the Bible for All Its Worth*, 132.
[8] Ronald F. Youngblood (ed.), *Nelson's Illustrated Bible Dictionary: New and Enhanced Edition* (Nashville: Thomas Nelson Inc., 2014), 15. https://books.google.com.gh/books?id=_cEjBQAAQBAJ&pg=PA15&lpg=PA15&dq=

question to answer is this: Does Acts simply record the history of the early Church or the recorded events are meant to be understood as a model for the church now and all times? We suggest the following principles in dealing with this question.⁹

Firstly, no exegesis should lead to a contradiction in either doctrine or practice with other parts of Scripture. For example, the three different and mutually exclusive approaches—casting lots (Acts 1:26), delegating others to do the selection (Acts 6:1-6) and directly appointing after prayer and fasting (Acts 14:23) — of selecting leaders in the Church are not to be considered as contradictory. Neither should one method be elevated to an absolute.

Secondly, the exegete must distinguish between historical and instructive portions of the Bible. Narratives do not serve as normative unless this is stated explicitly. For example, we read that the early Christians sold their possessions and goods and shared the proceeds to meet the needs of others. There is no command anywhere to practice this today, even though selflessness and helping others is a constant Christian virtue taught in different parts of Scripture. On the other hand, Peter's call to the Jerusalem crowd to repent (Acts 2:38) is seen as occurring again and again in Acts [See 3:19 (Peter issues the command to repentance in his sermon); 8:22 (a call to Simon Magus to repent); 17:30 (Paul calls the people of Athens to repent) and 26:20 (Paul calls King Agrippa, a Gentile to repentance)]. This means that Peter was giving a command to all people everywhere when he tells the crowd at Pentecost to repent. The same can be said of the command to be baptized.

The third principle is that a "command or a practice in Acts can only be considered normative if it is reinforced elsewhere in the New Testament", especially in Jesus's teachings and the Epistles. John R. W. Stott rightly stated years ago that "What is described in Scripture as having happened to others is not necessarily intended for us."¹⁰ In Acts 15:29 we read, "You are to abstain from food sacrificed to idols, from blood, from the meat of strangled animals and from sexual immorality." Does this command apply to believers today? We apply the principle of reinforcement as follows. The command to stay away from sexual immorality is repeated in the teaching of Jesus (Matt. 5:32; 15:19; 19:9), in the Epistles (Rom 1:29; 1 Cor. 6:13, 18; 7:2; Gal 5:19; Eph. 5:3; Col 3:3; 1 Thess. 4:3) and in the Book of Revelation (2:21; 9:21). The numerous reinforcements make it abundantly clear that the Jerusalem decree regarding

---

⁹ Stephen Voorwinde, "How Normative Is Acts?" in *Vox Reformata* 2010, (33-56'), 39-46.
¹⁰ John R. W. Stott, *Baptism and Fullness: The Work of the Holy Spirit Today,* 3rd edition (Leicester: Inter-Varsity Press, 2006), 21. https://books.google.com.gh/books?id=0hD3 bJB2XUUC&pg=PA21&lpg=PA21&dq

sexual immorality was intended to be a universal principle. The command to abstain from blood and the meat of strangled animals does not appear again either in Acts or anywhere else in the New Testament and so it seems safe to conclude that the decree was meant entirely for the Gentile believers to abstain from food sacrificed to idols at the time. In his letter to the Corinthians, Paul had the opportunity to reinforce it (1 Cor. 8-10) but did not do so. He took the view that meat sacrificed to idols can be blessed and eaten by Christians whose faith is strong but if that action tends to jeopardize the security of a believer with weak faith, then it should be avoided.

Epistles

An epistle is a form of written communication to an individual, group, or public audience. New Testament epistles include 1 and 2 Corinthians; Romans; Galatians; Ephesians; Philippians; Colossians; Philemon; 1 and 2 Thessalonians; 1 and 2 Timothy; Titus; Hebrews; James; 1 and 2 Peter; 1, 2, and 3 John, and Jude.

New Testament epistles have some common characteristic features. Firstly, they are characterized by a five-fold structure: opening address, greeting, prayer wish or thanksgiving, body of text, and closure. Secondly, they are pastoral responses to problems and situations in the church rather than systematic treatises. In some cases, the letters were written because the authors had received some questions from their audiences and needed to respond to them. Major issues addressed include false teachings. In Galatians, for example, Paul fights against a false teaching that insisted that the Galatian Christians must submit to circumcision in order to be right with God. In Colossians, Paul deals with the erroneous assumption that people must pass through a hierarchy of spirit beings before getting to Christ who is at the top of the hierarchy. Thirdly, most ancient letters were composed by secretaries.[11] Paul, an educated Jew, also used secretaries (see Rom. 16:22). Silas helped Peter in writing his letter (1 Pet. 5:12). Fourthly, they were written to be read in public not only because of the high illiteracy rate that characterized the first century, which made oral communication more effective than any other method but also because the letters were written to address ecclesiastical problems, for which reason it was necessary to read them in the church to the hearing of everyone (see Col. 4: 16).

Exegesis of New Testament epistles may be carried out with the following principles in mind.

---

[11] Mark L. Strauss, *How to Read the Bible in Changing Times: Understanding and Applying God's Word Today* (Grand Rapids, MI: Baker Books, 2011), 183.

1. The general historical context of the first-century church must be studied. The exegete must try to reconstruct the life situation that necessitated a particular epistle in order to determine the historical context of a particular teaching. For example, there is the need to know the historical-cultural underpinning to Paul's request that the Romans should greet themselves with the "holy kiss" (Rom. 16:16).

2. The socio-cultural context of the letter must be studied in order to determine which instructions are culturally conditioned and which ones are not. Should the instruction to women to cover their hair have a universal application?

3. The purpose of the letter must also guide the exegete to determine and appreciate the author's choice of words and style. The following questions are related to the purpose of the letter.

    i. Why is the author writing the letter?

    ii. What situation does the author face while writing his letter?

    iii. What problems does the author address in the letter?

    iv. What does the epistle tell us about the recipients?

    v. What is the author's attitude as revealed in the epistle?

    vi. What are the specific things mentioned about the specific occasion?

4. Study the literary context of the text following closely the progress of the author's argument. It is a good practice to read the entire epistle at one sitting as this practice helps the reader to grasp the key themes developed in the letter and the author's flow of thought.

5. The transferability of biblical principles and practices to our culture may sometimes be problematic to the exegete. In what follows we suggest some principles that may be useful in determining which cultural practices and situations, commands, and precepts in the Bible are transferable to our culture and which ones are nontransferable.

    i. The exegete needs to understand the rationale behind a command or custom in a given text. If the reason is rooted in God's unchanging nature, then it must be regarded as having a permanent relevance for people of all ages. Such a situation, command or principle is repeatable, continuous, and therefore is permanent and transferable to us (examples include Gen. 9:6; Prov. 3:5-6; John 3:3; Rom. 12:1-2; 1 Cor. 12:13; Eph. 6:10-19; Col. 3:12-13; 1 Pet. 5:6).

ii. Situations, commands, or principles that pertain to an individual's specific non-repeatable circumstances, or non-moral or non-theological subjects, or have been revoked, are not to be transferred to us. Examples are Matthew 21:2-3; 2 Timothy 4:11, 13; Hebrews 7:12; 10:1; Leviticus 20:11 (cf. 1 Cor. 5). In addition, all practices that were integral part of the surrounding pagan communities must be rejected.

iii. Some situations or commands remain as a permanent requirement for all times, but the actual application has no similarities to ours. Examples are Matthew 26:7; John 13:12-16; Exodus 3:5; Romans 16:16; 1 Corinthians 8; Deuteronomy 6:4-6. In such cases the exegete needs to modify the cultural forms but retain the content.

The Apocalypse

Apocalyptic literature (of both Testaments) shares certain common features. The first feature is that the apocalypse comprises the revelatory communication of heavenly secrets by an otherworldly being to the writer who presents the visions and sometimes their interpretations in a narrative. More so, Apocalyptic Literature is characterized by a dualistic, or two-world (this world and the other world) view of things. Apocalyptic Literature makes a clear distinction between good and evil, it portrays the power and the dark chaos that evil brings and also the power of God to ultimately overcome all evil. Literary imagery that shows contrast/dualism includes light and darkness, hideous and beautiful, above and below (See Daniel 7).

Furthermore, the Apocalypse contains other-worldly journeys which usually allow the writer (in this journey) to share in the mysteries of what God will finally do with the universe. In 1 Enoch 14:8 for example, the writer is taken through "the course of the stars and the lightings... high up into heaven." Usually, the visionary material comprises three major elements: the description of the setting (see Rev. 1:1-11); the record of the vision; (see Rev. 1:12-17); and the interpretation of the vision (see Rev. 1:11-20). Again, the Apocalypse also involves angels and other intermediaries who explain things to the writer. In Revelation, John is shown things by angels (1:1; 22:8) and by the "Son of Man," Christ himself (1:10-20). Fifth, Apocalyptic Literature is full of symbolism and

Literary Analysis 41

imagery (See Is. 6:6–7; Amos 7:1–8:3). In addition, numbers are also used to communicate the message which the writer seeks to convey to the readers (See Rev. 1:4, 7 churches; 7:4, 144,000 people sealed; 10:15, 7 angels).

The exegetical principles that emerge from the nature of Apocalyptic Literature are as follows:

1. Do not treat the material in an apocalypse in a strict chronological manner. Rather it must be treated topically. In Revelations 6, the world seems to have come to an end, but in chapter 8 more catastrophes are reported (see 6:13; 8:12; and 12:4).

2. Avoid adding to the interpretation that the intermediary gives.

3. In the case of Revelation, the interpreter must take into consideration the various kinds of genres it contains.[12] Prophecy must be interpreted as prophecy; the letter must be interpreted as letter and so on. Again, Christ must be seen as the central character in the whole book and as such a Christocentric exegesis must be carried out.

4. Any interpretation given in the text must be taken seriously and used as a starting point for the interpretation of the other parts.

Conclusion

After the introductory chapter, the study began a journey through the basic elements of biblical exegesis. We have seen in this chapter that the Bible contains different literary forms (genres) and each form is interpreted differently from the others. This chapter has brought to an end our discussions on the basic elements of Biblical Exegeses. Most of the things discussed in the chapters that follow are applications of these elements. The exegete must take each element seriously. However, not all of these elements may apply to a particular text. For example, there may be no serious textual problem with a text and so the step involving textual criticism may not apply. The exegete is therefore required to apply them as and when it is necessary. However, irrespective of the nature of the text and genre involved the contextual analysis and grammatical analysis cannot be ignored.

---

[12] Warren Jr., *Interpreting Apocalyptic Literature* in Bruce Corley, Steve W. Lemke and Grant I. Lovejoy, *Biblical Hermeneutics*, second edition (Tennessee: Broadman Publishers, 2002), 353.

Review Exercise

1. Critique the use of imprecatory prayers in contemporary churches.

2. How transferable is the practice of "holy kiss" (Rom. 16:16) to your society?

3. What message does Revelation 13 have for the 21st century church?

4. Does the Bible teach that only 144000 people will go to heaven (cf. Rev. 7:1-9)? Explain your answer.

5. How are we to interpret Biblical Epistles? Apply the principles stated above to 1 Corinthians 7.

6. Attempt an exegesis of Genesis 2:15. What lessons can we learn from your study in relation to environmental stewardship?

7. Through an exegetical analysis, explain how Jesus fulfills the Law according to Matthew 5:17.

8. Attempt an exegesis of Matthew 5:17-20 bringing out clearly the kind of righteousness required for Kingdom citizenship. Attempt an exegetical commentary on Deuteronomy 15:1-7. What theology of poverty can you formulate from your exegetical study?

9. Examine the role of alms giving, fasting and prayer in the exegesis of Matthew 6.

10. Attempt an exegesis of Matthew 6:12a.

11. Attempt an exegesis of Matthew 10, identifying five principles of mission in the text.

12. Explain the exegetical connection between Matthew 5:20 and Matthew 13.

13. Discuss the exegetical implications of Matthew 18.

14. Attempt an exegesis of Matthew 23:23, explaining clearly Jesus teaching about tithing according to this verse.

15. Does the command for women to cover their hair in church (1 Cor. 11:2-16) apply to Christians today?

Chapter 6

Socio-Rhetorical Biblical Interpretation

Socio-rhetorical biblical exegesis comes under a combination of socio-scientific method and rhetorical method of studying Scripture. In chapter one, we dealt briefly with social-scientific approach to biblical exegesis. We have dedicated this chapter to this interpretative approach because of its growing popularity and its effectiveness in discovering the different aspects of meaning of biblical texts. The term "socio-rhetorical" suggests at least two things. Firstly, the prefix "socio" suggests the search for an anthropological and sociological understanding of the society in which the Bible text was written.[1] Secondly, the term "rhetorical" points to the way language in a text serves as a means of communication among people; that is "the subjects and topics a text uses to present thought, speech, stories and arguments"[2] Socio-rhetorical interpretation is therefore an approach that combines people's ways of communication with their ways of life[3] by making use of data from various fields such as linguistics (inner texture), literary comparative (intertexture), social and historical (social and cultural texture), the ideology of the text (ideological texture) and the theology of the text regarding God and human (theological/sacred texture). Combining these methods is essential because, as Robbins observes, the independent use of each of them produces limited results, but when used interactively, the results are richer and more reflective of a responsible reading.[4] As Robbins, the founder of this approach has noted, socio-rhetorical analysis is based on the basic assumption that the meaning of a text does not depend only on the creative genius of its author but also on the relationship between a text and the contexts in which a text has been read and reread.

Historical Overview of Socio-Rhetorical Interpretation

Rhetorical criticism is often considered a recent addition to the field of Biblical Studies, but its application to biblical texts is not new. Scholars trace the history

---

[1] Vernon K. Robbins, *Exploring the Texture of Text: A Guide to Socio-Rhetorical Interpretation* (Valley Forge, PA: Trinity Press International, 1996), 1.
[2] Mack as cited in Robbins, *Exploring*, 1.
[3] Robbins, *Exploring*, 1.
[4] Robbins, *Exploring*, 2.

of the use of rhetorical approach to the study of the New Testament to the early Church Fathers. Janet Fairweather gives evidence of Chrysostom's use of rhetorical criticism to study Galatians.[5] Augustine also "finds the rhetoric of the Bible not that of paganism, but another equally qualitative variety suited to its authors and the importance of the subject matter."[6] He studied Paul's letters (example Galatians) using rhetorical analysis.[7]

Reformers such as Martin Luther and Philip Melanchthon also applied rhetoric to the New Testament. Melanchthon wrote rhetorical commentaries on Romans and Galatians.[8] Moreover, "Erasmus...provided rhetorical analyses of 1 and 2 Corinthians.... Calvin...besides noting rhetorical features (particularly stylistic) throughout his commentaries on the New Testament gives a rhetorical analysis of Romans."[9] In the late 16th century, a remarkable number of publications were made on both rhetoric and hermeneutics of Scripture.[10] From the time of the Church Fathers to the time of the Reformers, rhetorical analyses were restricted to stylistic matters, especially figures of speech and thought, and matters of genre and form. From the late 18th to the early 20th centuries, Germany became the center of rhetorical analysis of the New Testament. Karl Ludwig Bauer's analysis of Paul's use of classical rhetorical techniques stood tall among other works.[11] Emphasis in this era was largely on correctness, style, and the aesthetic appreciation of literature.[12]

Later, as other methodologies of biblical analysis emerged, interest in rhetorical analysis declined (probably due to the limited usefulness of stylistic studies). Wuellner records that, "[w]ith the rise of historical (scientific or modern) criticism, rhetoric became marginalized to the point of near

---

[5] Janet Fairweather, "The Epistle to the Galatians and Classical Rhetoric," *TynBul* 45 (1994): 1.

[6] Duane F. Watson and Alan J. Hauser, *Rhetorical Criticism of the Bible: A Comprehensive Bibliography with Notes on History and Method* (E. J. Brill Leiden: New York· Koln, 1994), 101.
https://books.google.com.gh/books?id=7IhAb1ZHfp0C&pg=PA102&lpg=PA102&dq

[7] Saint Augustine, *On Christian Doctrine*, translated by D. W. Robertson (New York: The Liberal Arts Press, 07/04/19 1958), 4.4.6. Wilhelm Wuellner, "Hermeneutics and Rhetorics: From 'Truth and Method' to 'Truth and Power'" *Scriptura* S 3 (1989): 3.

[8] Watson and Hauser, *Rhetorical Criticism of the Bible*, 102.

[9] Watson and Hauser, *Rhetorical Criticism of the Bible*, 102-103.

[10] Wuellner, "Hermeneutics and Rhetorics," 11, citing Deborah Shuger, "Morris Croll, Flacius Illyricus, and the Origin of Anti-Ciceronianism," *Rhetorica* 3 (1985): 280.

[11] See Watson and Hauser, *Rhetorical Criticism*, 103.

[12] Jack R. Lundbom, *Jeremiah: A Study in Ancient Hebrew Rhetoric* (2nd ed.; Winona Lake, Ind.: Eisenbrauns, 1997), xx.

extinction or at least increasing irrelevance, in contrast to its fifteen hundred year-long central importance to exegesis."[13]

After years of its decline, rhetorical analysis was revived by the works of Amos Wilder and James Muilenburg. The renewed interest in rhetorical studies came as a result of a general dissatisfaction with form and redaction criticisms.[14] Wilder applied rhetorical analysis to the New Testament using early Christian rhetoric. His work served as a motivation for Vernon K. Robbins who later developed socio-rhetorical interpretation. In his 1955 presentation to the Society of Biblical Literature (SBL), Wilder discussed "the nature of religious symbol and symbolic discourse, referred to New Testament eschatology as 'a tremendous expression of the religious imagination, an extraordinary rhetoric of faith', and encouraged the use of insights from the fields of cultural anthropology and folklore to interpret biblical literature."[15] He challenged interpreters to focus their research on analysis that was grounded in, and attentive to the rhetorical, literary and linguistic dimensions of early Christian texts.

Muilenberg, an Old Testament scholar with a background in classics and literature, in his 1968 presidential address to the SBL, protested that overemphasis on the use of Form Criticism has resulted in the neglect of the actual content of the Bible. He challenged biblical scholars to move Biblical Studies beyond Form Criticism and into what he then termed "rhetorical criticism."[16] While the methods proposed by Muilenburg were not new, his address encouraged scholars to work consciously with Rhetorical Criticism when engaging biblical texts. Muilenburg's speech provided the definition, direction and impetus for this approach to the Scripture. Despite his impressive contribution to rhetorical analysis, Muilenburg could not fully develop a methodology of interpretation which integrated the language of the text itself with its subsequent effect on audiences.

---

[13] Wilhelm Wuellner, "Rhetorical Criticism and Its Theory in Culture-Critical Perspective: The Narrative Rhetoric of John 11" in *Text and Interpretation: New Approaches in the Criticism of the New Testament* edited by P. J. Hartin and J. H. Petzer (Leiden: Brill, 1991), 174.
[14] Watson and Hauser, *Rhetorical Criticism of the Bible*, 102.
[15] Vernon K. Robbins, *The Tapestry of Early Christian Discourse: Rhetoric, Society and Ideology* (London and New York: Routledge, 2003), 2.
[16] James Muilenburg, "Form Criticism and Beyond," *JBL* 88 (1969).

Robbins' 1975 article entitled "The We-Passages in Acts and Ancient Sea Voyages"[17] gave birth to socio-rhetorical criticism. In this work, Robbins contended for a strong correlation between the way people use language and the way they live in the "we-passages" of Acts. To substantiate his argument, Robbins explained that traveling in a boat on the sea with other people created a social environment that made it natural for some authors in antiquity to use the first person plural ("we") for literary accounts of sea voyages. He added that this phenomenon represented a cultural intertexture of sea voyages that dates back to Homer's Odyssey. Robbins followed this article with his 1984 publication *Jesus the Teacher: A Socio-Rhetorical Interpretation of Mark* in which the term "socio-rhetorical" was first introduced into New Testament studies. Since then he has been at the forefront of the developments within socio-rhetorical analysis.[18] In the 1992 "New Introduction" which appeared in the Paperback Edition of this pioneering work, Robbins explains that he was trying to work "toward a method that brought information about Mediterranean society and culture into interpretation of Gospels and Acts."[19] Robbins, in 1996, outlined a method of socio-rhetorical analysis entitled *Exploring the Texture of Texts: A Guide to Socio-Rhetorical Interpretation*, a work which remains the standard introduction to the field despite its complicated nature. Robbins adopted the approach of a cultural anthropologist in his interpretation and contended that both the "formalist approach to the text and the use of sociology without the rich resources of social and cultural anthropology limit the studies to a conventional view of the historical and social nature of early Christianity."[20] Robbins' socio-rhetorical approach utilizes "rhetorical analysis and interpretation that is based on both oral and literary dynamics within social, cultural, ideological, and religious contexts of interaction during the first century CE to interpret New Testament literature."[21]

---

[17] Vernon K. Robbins, "The We-Passages in Acts and Ancient Sea Voyages" in *Perspectives on Luke-Acts*, ed. C.H. Talbert (Edinburgh: T & T Clark, 1978), 215-42.
[18] David B. Gowler, "Socio-Rhetorical Interpretation: Textures of a Text and its Reception" in *Journal for the Study of the New Testament* 33(2) 191-206, 2010: 191.
[19] Vernon K. Robbins, *Jesus the Teacher: A Socio-Rhetorical Interpretation of Mark* (Philadelphia: Fortress, 1992), xix.
[20] Robbins, *Jesus the Teacher*, xxi.
[21] Vernon Robbins, *The Invention of Christian Discourse*, I (Blandford Forum, UK: Deo Publishing, 2009), 3.

Framework for Socio-Rhetorical Interpretation

Socio-Rhetorical Interpretation, as developed by Robbins, requires that a text be analyzed from five different perspectives or "textures", namely, the inner texture, the intertexture, the social and cultural texture, the ideological texture and the theological/sacred texture. This is because Robbins noted that a text can be viewed as a rich tapestry of textures each of which represents meaning in a unique way. We shall outline each of these textures briefly below.

Inner Texture

Inner texture refers to the use of words in a text as tools of communication. It involves "the repetition of particular words, the creation of beginnings and endings, alternation of speech and storytelling, particular ways in which the words present arguments, and the particular 'feel' or aesthetic of the text."[22] Inner textural analysis comes before the "real interpretation" of the text.[23] This means that before the reader tries to determine the meaning of the text he/she must be careful to find out what the text is about and what it says in order to recognize its shape and form. The interpreter is required to put aside all of his/her presumptions about what the text is about, and instead allow the text itself to show its topics in the form of lexical indicators, narrative characters, forms of action, temporal and spatial settings and so on. It is only after the shape of the text is discovered that the interpreter can begin to recognize how the words, phrases, sentences, and paragraphs join together to form the meaning of the text. This analysis is conducted in order "to gain an intimate knowledge of words, word patterns, voices, structures, devices, and modes in the text, which are the context for meanings and meaning-effects that an interpreter analyzes with the other readings of the text."[24]

Robbins identifies six types of inner texture in a text, namely repetitive, progressive, opening-middle-closing, narrational, argumentative, and sensory-aesthetic textures. Repetitive texture, examines the occurrence of a word or phrases for more than once in a unit as well as "grammatical, syntactical, verbal, or topical phenomena."[25] Example of repetition texture occurs in the Matthean Beatitudes where the word blessed is repeated nine times (v. 3, 4, 5, 6, 7, 8, 9, 10 and 11). A common repetitive structure in Greco-Roman literature is *inclusio*, "envelope figure" or "ring composition" where the opening words are repeated

---

[22] Robbins, *Exploring*, 3.
[23] Robbins, *Tapesty*, 7.
[24] Robbins, *Exploring*, 7.
[25] Robbins, *Exploring*, 8.

or paraphrased at the close. An example of *inclusio* occurs in Philippians 1:3-11 through the repetition of the word God in v.3 and v.11. Another common repetitive rhetorical structure is called chiasm which occurs when an author introduces two or more elements followed by the presentation of corresponding elements in reverse order. Matthew 6:24 presents as a five-part chiasm:

    A No one can serve two masters,

        B for either he will hate the one,

            C and love the other,

            C' or he will be devoted to the one.

        B' and despise the other.

    A' You cannot serve God and money.

Progressive texture has to do with the sequence of words throughout a unit. Though progressive texture grows out of repetitive texture, repetitive texture requires the reader to simply collect repetitive elements while progressive texture requires him/her to discover any sequences that unfold along with the repetitive elements. For example, in James 1:2-8, the key ideas progress from joy/trials to complete/lack to asking/giving to faith/doubting to receiving/not receiving.

Opening-middle-closing texture, examines the beginning, body and conclusion of the unit. For narratives, this texture usually (but not always) corresponds to the opening, middle and closing of a story's plot, or the opening, middle, closing of a speech given by a narrative character.

Narrational texture focuses on prominent narrative elements of a text such as characters and their actions, spatial and temporal settings, and events. It distinguishes between real author, implied author, narrator, characters, narratee, implied reader and real reader.

Argumentative texture, deals with the nature of the argument in a unit. Rhetorical argumentation relies upon social logic, and until the relevant elements of this logic are discovered in intertextural analysis, it will be possible to examine only the surface level argumentative structure of the text rather than its full argumentative force. A rhetorical argument functions through either deductive or inductive argumentation, and is delivered through either the explicit words of the text (rhetology), or through cognitive linkages formed through those mental images that have been evoked by the text (rhetography). An example of deductive rhetorical argumentation from Matthew 6:24 is as follows:

Premise: "No servant can serve two masters;"

Rationale: "for either he will hate the one and love the other, or he will be devoted to the one and despise the other."

Conclusion: "You cannot serve God and mammon" (cf. Luke 16:13).

The argumentative mode is deductive in Luke because it argues through mutual exclusivity: what is "false" cannot at the same time be "true." Inductive rhetorical argumentation draws inferences through linkages other than those found in quasi-logical argumentation. Paul's confrontation with a group of disciples in Ephesus about their baptism in Acts 19 is an example of an "ends and means" inductive argument. Here, Paul argues that John's baptism was a means intended to facilitate the "end" of baptism "in the name of Jesus Christ."

Sensory-aesthetic texture identifies and groups every aspect of a text that refers to a part of the body—ears, eyes, hands, feet, stomach and so on. It deals with both the range of senses evoked by the text as well as the manner in which they are evoked.[26] Robbins distinguishes three "body zones" that can be found in a text that reflects how human beings interact with their environment.[27] The zone of emotion-fused thought concerns the eyes and heart. Examples of verbs, nouns, and adjectives that belong to this zone include: to see, to understand, intelligence, hatred, sadness, love, foolishness, jealousy, joyousness and others. In James 3:16 words such as envy, self-seeking, confusion are examples of emotion-fused thoughts. The zone of self-expressive speech concerns the mouth and ears. Examples of verbs, nouns, and adjectives that belong to this zone include: to say, to hear, to sing, attentiveness, voice, sound, and silent/silence. The zone of purposeful action concerns the hands and feet. Verbs, nouns, and adjectives that belong to this zone include: to hit, to walk, to touch, gesture, behavior, activity, quick, and others.

Intertexture

Robbins defines intertexture as "…a text's representation of, reference to, and use of phenomena in the 'world' outside of the text being interpreted. … [It] is the interaction of the language in the text with 'outside' material and physical "objects," historical events, texts, customs, values, institutions and systems."[28] Analysis of intertexture includes oral-scribal intertexture, cultural intertexture, historical intertexture and social intertexture. It focuses on a passage's use of

---

[26] Robbins, *Exploring*, 29-30.
[27] Robbins, *Exploring*, 30.
[28] Robbins, *Tapestry*, 40.

texts outside of itself. To achieve this, the interpreter looks out for recitation, recontextualization, reconfiguration and thematic elaboration. Recitation refers to the transmission of a story, from oral or written form, in the "exact words."[29] Recitation ranges from the replication of exact words to the utilization of different words in a variety of forms (on a spectrum from most of the words being the same to reciting the narrative in substantially one's own words) all the way to the more general summarization of the previous text (s). The statement "Do not murder" in Matthew 5:21b is the exact recitation of Exodus 20:13.

Recontextualization includes the presentation of wording from previous texts without an explicit acknowledgment that these words/texts exist in another text and are being (re)used. 1 Peter 2.3 is a good example of recontextualization of Psalm 34.8. The Petrine passage reads: "Like newborn babes, long for the pure spiritual milk, that by it you may grow up to salvation; *for you have tasted the kindness of the Lord.*" Here, Peter puts words from Psalm 34.8 in a new context without telling the reader that the words stand in Scripture.

Reconfiguration means restructuring an antecedent tradition.[30] In other words, it utilizes aspects of a previous event/situation to describe a later event in such a way that the former event appears to foreshadow the later event. The Adam-Christ typology of Romans 5:12-20 falls under this category. The way the writer of the gospel of Matthew introduces Jesus in the Sermon on the Mount (Matt. 5:1-2) recalls how Moses gave the Commandments to the Israelites on Mount Sinai (Ex. 19ff). Jesus "opens his mouth" and instructs the people in a similar way Moses instructed the Israelites. Jesus is presented as the new Moses giving "new" Torah. This makes what Jesus says very important and authoritative for his audience.

Narrative amplification expands a brief narrative into a longer and more complex form, and this extended composition often integrates recitation, recontextualization and/or reconfiguration.[31] Thematic elaboration takes a theme or issue from an earlier text and elaborates on that theme by utilizing modes of rhetorical argumentation. Paul's discourse about death and resurrection in early Christian discourse (1 Cor. 15) is an example of thematic elaboration in that Paul explains further two themes (death and resurrection) which were already part of Christian discourse.

Cultural intertexture refers to "the logic of a particular culture," be it an extensive culture essentially co-extensive with the boundaries of an empire, or

---

[29] Robbins, *Tapestry*, 102.
[30] Robbins, *Tapestry*, 107.
[31] Robbins, *Exploring*, 51.

a 'local' culture.[32] Cultural intertexture focuses on the "insider" knowledge readers have about a particular society and culture. Historical intertexture deals with events that have occurred at particular times and places.[33] It includes the social, cultural and ideological backgrounds of the text.[34] It differs from social intertexture by its focus on a particular event or period of time rather than social practices that occur regularly as events in one's life. A careful consideration of the "limited information about a historical event" is required to obtain reliable results.[35] Finally, Social intertexture is concerned with the meaning and effects of certain social practices that are common to the entire society.

Social and Cultural Texture

Social and cultural texture refers to a situation whereby a text interacts with society and culture by sharing in the general social and cultural attitudes, norms and modes of interaction that are known by everyone in a society, and by establishing itself in relationship with the dominant cultural system as either sharing, rejecting or transforming those attitudes, values and dispositions.[36] Social and cultural texture "concerns the capacities of the text to support social reform, withdrawal, or opposition and to evoke cultural perceptions of dominance, subordinance, difference, or exclusion."[37] This would include the text's attempts to persuade or influence the audience.

According to Robbins, social and cultural texture uses anthropological and social theory to explore the social and cultural nature of the voices in the text and this makes it different from intertextural analysis. [38] This deals with the "social and cultural 'location' of the language and the type of social or cultural world that language creates."[39] To this end, the reader looks out for evidence in the text, or those known through historical and anthropological research, of cultural and social practices that are not readily apparent to him/her in contemporary cultures. There are three parameters of social and cultural

---

[32] Robbins, *Tapestry*, 129.
[33] Robbins, *Tapestry*, 117.
[34] Robbins, *Exploring*, 63.
[35] Robbins, *Exploring*, 63-64.
[36] Vernon K. Robbins, "Socio-rhetorical Interpretation," http://www.religion.emory.edu/faculty/robbins/SRI/index.cf
[37] Robbins, *Exploring*, 3.
[38] Robbins, *Tapestry*, 144.
[39] Robbins, *Tapestry*, 144.

texture, namely, "specific social topics, common social and cultural topics, and final categories."[40]

Specific social topics analyzes the language of the passage being studied in order to identify the worldview that it evokes. It includes thoughts, ideas, and subjects that are central to a particular kind of social discourse. Robbins looks at seven different cultural responses that may be created by a religious text through the language it employs. What follows is a summary of these cultural responses as given by W. Randolph Tate.

1. The *conversionist* response views the world as corrupt because all people are corrupt: if people can change, then the world will be changed.

2. The *revolutionist* response assumes that only the destruction of the world—more specifically, of the social order— will suffice to save people.

3. The *introversionist* response sees the world as irredeemably evil and presupposes that salvation can be attained only by the fullest possible withdrawal from it.

4. The *gnostic (manipulationist)* response seeks only a transformed set of relationships—a transformed method of coping with evil— since salvation is possible in the world if people learn the right means, improved techniques, to deal with their problems.

5. The *thaumaturgical* response focuses on the concern of individual people to receive specific dispensations for relief from present and specific ills.

6. The *reformist* response assumes that people may create an environment of salvation in the world by using supernaturally given insights to change the present social organization into a system that functions toward good ends.

7. The *utopian* response presupposes that people must take an active and constructive role in replacing the entire present social system with a new social organization in which evil is absent.[41]

---

[40] Robbins, *Exploring*, 71.

Common social and cultural topics include topics that are familiar to the social and cultural systems and institutions of the audience. That is, the values, world views and beliefs of the world that gave birth to the writing of the biblical text.[42] This stage of the analysis enables the reader to develop an unbiased understanding of the passage in order that he/she might not get a different view of it due to his/her modern/postmodern experiences. Some of these cultural issues are honor, shame, legal contracts, challenge–response (riposte), economic exchange, and purity codes that are related to the first-century Greco-Roman society. Each of the ministry gifts in Ephesians 4:11 are common social/cultural topics.[43] For example, the first ministry gift listed, apostle, has significant meaning for the first-century church. In Hebrews, Jesus is referred to as the apostle (*tón apóstolon*) and the High Priest of our confession. In Jesus' day, the word *apostle* was used often, mostly in reference to the twelve disciples (Luke 6:13). Though the word apostle is not found in the Old Testament, the idea of a "sent one" is found. God sent the prophet Nathan to rebuke David for committing sin with Uriah's wife and masterminding the murder of Uriah as well (1 Sam. 12). God also sent Moses to the Egyptian King Pharaoh (Ex. 3-12). By Jesus' time the term *apostéllō* generally referred to the sending of a fleet or embassy, but Epictetus also used the term to describe Zeus sending a teacher of philosophy as his messenger. It was therefore a term common to his audience based on the socio-cultural setting.

The final cultural category focuses on the cultural location of a reader, writer, or the text.[44] By cultural location we mean the way people present propositions, reasons, and arguments both to themselves and to others. It deals with "the manner in which people present their propositions, reasons, and arguments both to themselves and to other people (i.e., rhetoric)."[45] Once the cultural location (in contrast to the social location) of a reader or writer is determined the dispositions, prepositions, and values which influence the writing and reading of a text becomes revealing.

---

[41] See W. Randolph Tate, *Handbook for Biblical Interpretation: An Essential Guide to Methods, Terms, and Concepts* (Grand Rapids, MI: Baker Academic, 2012), 415.
[42] Robbins, *Exploring*, 75.
[43] For exhaustive treatment of this text consult Jimmy D. Bayes, "Five-fold Ministry: A Social and Cultural Texture Analysis of Ephesians 4:11-16" in *Journal of Biblical Perspectives in Leadership* 3, no. 1 (Winter 2010), 113-122. The example that follows was gleaned from Bayes' work.
[44] Robbins, *Exploring*, 86.
[45] Jimmy D. Bayes, "Five-fold Ministry: A Social and Cultural Texture Analysis of Ephesians 4:11-16" in *Journal of Biblical Perspectives in Leadership* 3, no. 1 (Winter 2010), 113-122, 121.

According to Robbins, final cultural categories may be classified into dominant culture, subculture, counterculture, contra-culture, and luminal culture.[46] Dominant culture represents "a system of attitudes, values, dispositions, and norms" that the speaker either presumes or asserts are "supported by social structures vested with power to impose its goal in a significantly broad territorial region."[47] It may be either indigenous or conquering cultures.

The term subculture may represent "the cultural patterns of a subsociety which contains both sexes, all ages, and family groups, and which parallels the larger society in that it provides for a network of groups and institutions extending throughout the individual's entire life cycle."[48] The subculture imitates the attitudes, values, dispositions and norms of the dominant culture and claims to enact them better than the members of dominant status. Subcultures differ from one another according to the prominence of one of three characteristics, namely, a network of communication and loyalty (in which "a chain of communication and loyalty among certain individuals, families and institutions is the most prominent feature"), a conceptual system (which is "a system of basic presuppositions about life, the world and nature is the most prominent feature") and ethnic heritage and identity (which originates from a language different from that of the dominant culture).[49]

Counterculture arises from a dominant culture and/or subculture and yet rejects the explicit and mutable characteristics of the dominant or subculture rhetoric to which it responds. Counterculture rhetoric evokes the creation of a "better society" not by force or legislation, but by offering alternatives and hopes that the society will "see the light" and adopt a more humanistic way of life. It differs from subculture in that while subculture affirms the national culture and the fundamental value orientation of the dominant society, a counter-culture rejects the norms and values which make the dominant culture a united entity.[50]

Contraculture rhetoric is a short-lived, counterculture deviance, primarily a reaction–formation response to a dominant culture, subculture, or counterculture.[51] Contracultures are "groups that do not involve more than one generation, which do not elaborate a set of institutions that allow the

---

[46] Robbins, *Tapestry*, 168ff.
[47] Robbins, *Tapestry*, 168.
[48] See Robbins, *Tapestry*, 168.
[49] Robbins, *Tapestry*, 168-169.
[50] See Robbins, *Tapestry*, 170.
[51] See Robbins, *Tapestry*, 170.

group to be relatively autonomous and self-sufficient, and which do not sustain an individual over an entire life span."[52] Predictions of the behavior and values in contraculture is possible if one knows the values of the society, sub-society or counter-society to which it is reacting, since the values are simply negated. Members of contra-culture therefore inherently have more negative than positive ideas.

Liminal culture rhetoric lasts only momentarily. Liminal culture appears and disappears as people move from one cultural identity to another, or consists of people or groups that have never been able to establish a clear social and cultural identity in their setting.[53] The language of a liminal culture is characterized by a "dialectic of culture and identification" that has neither binary nor hierarchical clarity.

The final cultural dimension determines a text's cultural location. Cultural location concerns the manner in which people present their propositions, reasons, and arguments to themselves and others. Subcultures differ from one another according to the prominence of a network of communication and loyalty, a conceptual system, and ethnic heritage and identity. The most prominent feature of a conceptual subculture is their basic assumptions of life, the world, and nature. We learn from his epistles that Paul is not preaching to reform the world or the Mediterranean culture, but is preaching a diversion from the Gentile world ("you should no longer walk as the rest of the Gentiles walk, in the futility of their mind," Eph. 4:17b). Being different from the world is the goal. It is through the ministry gifts that the church will be able to change the world.

Ideological Texture

Ideological texture involves the way that the author and readers position themselves in relation to other individuals and groups. Ideological texture, as Robbins notes, concerns the particular alliances and conflicts nurtured and evoked by the language of the text and the language of the interpretation as well as the way the text itself and interpreters of the text position themselves in relation to other individuals and groups.

Every text and every interpretation of a text has an ideology which refers to the particular alliances and conflicts nurtured and evoked by the language of the text and of the interpretation. Ideological texture has to do with the way the text itself and its readers see themselves in relation to other individuals

---

[52] Robbins quoting Roberts in *Tapestry*, 170.
[53] Robbins, *Tapestry*, 170.

and groups. Therefore, in order to analyze the ideological texture of a text one has to give attention to the social and cultural location of the implied author, the ideology of power in the text, as well as the ideology of the mode of discourse in a text. It also deals with the individual location of the individual reader, relations to groups within the text, modes of intellectual discourse, and spheres of ideology. For Robbins, "The beginning place for ideological analysis and interpretation is with people and the best place to begin is with you, the reader of this sentence."[54] Three ideological contexts, namely, the author's ideological context, the ideology reproduced by the text itself and the reader's ideological context have been identified by scholars.[55] Finally, one should be honest and own up to one's own social, cultural and ideological position and its possible impact on one's interpretation.

Sacred/Theological Texture

Robbins explains the nature and function of theological or sacred texture by saying, "people who read the New Testament regularly are interested in finding insights into the nature of the relation between human life and the divine. ... [They are] interested in locating the ways the text speaks about God ... or talks about realms of religious life."[56] This texture deals with the relationship between humans and the divine.[57] That is, it refers to the manner in which a text communicates insights into the relationship between the human and the divine. Here, the reader looks for sacred aspects of the text and for the divine nature.

To achieve this, the interpreter has to determine the text's reference to deity, holy person, spirit being, divine history, human redemption, human commitment, religious community, and ethics.[58] "These aspects of a text are embedded deeply in the inner texture, intertexture, social and cultural texture and ideological texture of a text."[59] Sacred texture concerns experience of special forces—whether good or evil; experience of divine control; guidance in social or personal history; or experience of human behavior that is shaped by encounters with the sacred. It often emerges in the context of conflict

---

[54] Robbins, *Exploring*, 96.
[55] As cited by Tate, *Handbook*, 416.
[56] Robbins, *Texture*, 120.
[57] Robbins, "Dictionary of Socio—Rhetorical Terms," Socio—rhetorical Interpretation. http://www.religion.emory.edu/faculty/robbins/SRI/defns/index.cfm (accessed on 24th August, 2016)
[58] Robbins, Exploring, 120-130.
[59] Robbins, *Tapestry*, 130.

between good and evil spiritual forces. The manner in which this battle is resolved sheds yet more light on the relation of human life to the divine in the text. An example of sacred texture can be found in Revelation 8 where God is depicted as judge over creation. This picture emerges in Revelation 8:1, and is strengthened by the symbolism in the heavenly throne room scene in Revelation 8.2-6. In the heavenly throne room scene of Revelation 8.2-6, God is the one who ultimately unleashes the trumpet plagues in response to the prayers of the saints.

Conclusion

In socio-rhetorical terms, a text may be likened to a thickly woven tapestry, which when viewed from different angles, exhibits different configurations, patterns and images. Socio-rhetorical criticism identifies five textures, namely, inner texture, intertexture, social and cultural texture, ideological texture and sacred texture, as different angles from which to approach the interpretive process. In so doing socio-rhetorical analysis creates an environment of 'invitation', dialogue and interaction among interpreters and between the multiple textures of a particular text.

Review Exercise

1. How would you differentiate between Socio-Rhetorical Interpretation and other methods of Biblical Interpretation?

2. Define the term "Rhetorical Criticism." Why is Rhetorical Criticism relevant?

3. Examine in detail each of the five textures of Socio-Rhetorical Interpretation.

4. What are the advantages of Socio-Rhetorical Interpretation?

5. Attempt a socio-rhetorical analysis of Matthew 6:19-24.

6. How does socio-rhetorical reading of the Matthean Beatitudes enhance our understanding of the text? Explain with relevant examples from the text.

7. What exegetical issues could be raised through the socio-rhetorical reading of Romans 13:1-7?

8. Attempt a socio-rhetorical interpretation of Matthew 28:16-20, explaining the place of teaching in the fulfillment of the Great Commission.

9. Attempt a socio-rhetorical interpretation of Hebrews 1:1-4. What are the implications of your study to African Christianity?

10. Through a socio-rhetorical reading of Romans 1:18-28, determine God's position on sexual orientation.

Chapter 7

African Biblical Studies (ABS)

In the introductory chapter, we noted that the gospel message can only be meaningful to African Christians if it touches on their everyday life experiences. This part of the book discusses African Biblical Studies (ABS) as an academic discipline. ABS is part of cultural hermeneutics which refers to the reading of a text from one's cultural perspective. The present chapter traces the historical development of ABS, noting its relevance and how Africans can benefit from it. The main contention of the chapter is that Africans will better understand and apply God's word to their lives if they read the Scriptures in an African way. In the last section of the chapter, we introduce readers to how an African scholar, Elizabeth Mburu proposes for the task of ABS to be carried out.

What is African Biblical Studies (ABS)?

The expression "African Biblical Studies" ("African Biblical Reading" or "African Biblical Exegesis or Hermeneutics") has been defined differently by different scholars. According to Aloo Osotsi Mojola, ABS refers to the study of the Bible from African perspective.[1] He means to say that, ABS is the use of contextual principles and approaches to elucidate the meaning of Scripture in a way that adequately addresses the socio-cultural issues of Africa. J. S. Ukpong is of the view that a biblical study that is called African is one that addresses African's needs through "an encounter between the Biblical text and the African context."[2] In the view of David Tuesday Adamo, ABS refers to a methodology of biblical interpretation that makes "African social cultural context a subject of interpretation"[3] or the rereading of the Bible from an Africentric perspective.[4] Adamo further notes that ABS "reappraises ancient

---

[1] AO Mojola, Interview by Isaac Boaheng at St. Paul's University, Limuru, Kenya on 24th January, 2019.
[2] J S Ukpong, "Developments in Biblical interpretation in Africa: Historical and hermeneutic directions" in *JTSA* 108, (2000) 3-18: 3.
[3] David Tuesday Adamo, "African Cultural Hermeneutics," *Vernacular Hermeneutics*, ed. Sugirtharajah (Sheffield: Sheffield Academic Press, 1999), 5.
[4] David Tuesday Adamo, *Explorations in African Biblical Studies* (Eugene, Oregon: Wipf & Stock Publishers, 2001), 6.

biblical tradition and African worldview, culture, and life experience with the purpose of 'correcting the effect of the cultural ideological conditioning to which Africa and Africans have been subjected.'"[5] A major fact deducible from the above definitions is that an African reading of Scripture is deeply rooted in the African worldview and culture. By "worldview" is meant "a mental model of reality, a framework of ideas and attitudes about the world, ourselves and life"[6] or "basic set of beliefs, or system of faith, or way of thinking is our worldview"[7] based on a person's inherited characteristics, attitudes, background, life experiences, values, habits and so on. A person's worldview informs his/her values and character.

The question of who qualifies to do ABS or what kind of work qualifies to be labeled ABS needs to be considered at this point. Is it the content of one's work, the identity of the researcher or both that determine what ABS is? Can non-Africans do ABS? According to Adamo, anyone doing ABS must be an insider; that is one who lives in Africa and has experienced life realities on the continent.[8] Those who have not experienced African realities like ethnicity, poverty, hunger, child labor, communal life, rites of passage, and others, do not qualify to do ABS. Adamo, therefore, believes it is the identity of the researcher (and his/her experience of African realities) rather than the content of a work that determines what work is to be labeled ABS or not.[9] If so, then a work by a European scholar who applies a biblical text to issues bothering Africans may not be classified as ABS, at the very least due to the fact that he/she has no personal experience of the African reality. Adamo, based on this reasoning, charges Africans to take the initiative to study the Bible for their own contexts.

Contrary to Adamo's claim, both Mojola and Ukpong maintain that it is the content of a work that determines whether it may be labeled ABS or not. In Ukpong's view, any work that integrates African elements into the historical and literary readings of the Bible in such a way as to arrive at distinct conclusions from those made by Western counterparts on the same texts may

---

[5] David T Adamo, "Decolonizing African Biblical Studies" Professorial Inaugural Lecture delivered at the Delta State University, Abraka, 3.
[6] Craig Rusbult, Worldview, http://www.asa3.org/ASA/education/views/index.html [Accessed 10 May, 2015]
[7] Jobe Martin, *The Evolution of a Creationist* (Texas: Biblical Discipleship Publishers, 2002), 22-2. (pdf)
[8] Adamo, *Exploration in African Biblical*, 5ff.
[9] This does not, however mean that any work done by an African is to be regarded ABS. Of course the content of a work is relevant in classifying it as ABS or not but the identity of the researcher comes first.

be classified as ABS.[10] Mojola contends that ABS is not limited to Africans because someone may be an African and not study the Bible from the African cultural lens while a non-African may engage a biblical text from the African viewpoint.[11] The determining factor is the perspective from which one engages the Scripture; an engagement of Scripture from an African worldview makes a work ABS, while a non-African reading of the Scripture disqualifies a work to be classified as ABS.[12]

In our candid opinion the content of one's work is the appropriate determinant for classifying it as ABS or not. The reason is that almost all the leading scholars advocating for an African reading of the Bible (including Adamo) have argued (explicitly or implicitly) that Africans engage in Western hermeneutics simply because they use Western methodologies in reading the Bible. If Africans (who are not Westerners) can do Western hermeneutics based on the use of Western-brewed methodologies, it stands to reason that non-Africans can also do ABS if the methodology used fits the African context. However, it is important that those who do ABS gain sufficient understanding (through personal experience, literary research or both) of the African indigenous culture and realities.

Certain conditions are necessary for doing ABS. Like any other theological exercise, one must have sufficient knowledge of the Bible (its language and culture), believe what it says and live by it in order to do a meaningful ABS.[13] If the goal of ABS is taken to be the desire to relate positively to the meaning of the text, then the most important factor is that the researcher needs to be a Christian. Being a Christian ensures that the person is connected to the Holy Spirit. The leading of the Holy Spirit will result in a positive response to the implications of the text. If however, the study is merely intended to produce meaning from the text, then the unbelieving researcher can equally welcome the task. The African situation makes it necessary for those doing ABS to believe not only in the existence of God but also in God's power to do and undo all things; that is God's ability to perform miracles. This aspect is very crucial because in Africa, religion is expected to respond to people's health, social needs and economic needs, to mention a few. This will inform the interpreters' discourse about God's power to deal with disease, poverty, oppression and conflict (among others) that characterize life on the African

---

[10] J. S. Ukpong, "Models and methods on Biblical interpretation in Africa", in *NeueZeitschrift fur Missionswissenschaft* 55 (1999), 279-295:281.
[11] Mojola, interview.
[12] Mojola, interview.
[13] Adamo, "Decolonizing African Biblical Studies", 8.

continent. In all, ABS has the potential of helping Africans to better apply the texts of the Bible to their existential situations.

Why an African Reading of the Bible?

The reasons for African's quest for a hermeneutical framework for Africa are not far-fetched. Firstly, research has shown that the African context has great potential that can enhance African understanding and interpretation of biblical texts. This fact is brought to bear when one compares the Hebrew culture to the African culture. As a matter of fact, the African worldview is closer to the biblical worldview than the European worldview and therefore Africans are in a better position to understand God's word if they would go directly to the text and engage it from their own perspective. Here are few examples. Sacrificial rituals found in Old Testament narratives and Jesus' sacrifice on the cross can more easily be appreciated by Africans who have seen sacrifices performed to gods than people from places where sacrifices are no more performed.[14] In addition, the celebration of elaborate funerals, the agricultural activities undertaken by ancient Jews, the purification rites for women during their monthly flows, the communal worldview, the practice of polygamy and other practices in the Old Testament are found in most indigenous African societies. Old Testament Wisdom Literature is more easily understood by African peoples because of their rich proverbial traditions. This is not to say that there are no discontinuities between the African culture and the biblical culture.

Secondly, the existence of different cultural settings makes it impossible to have a "uniform, unconditional, universal, and absolute interpretation or hermeneutics," as every interpreter "tends to bring his or her own bias to bear, consciously or unconsciously, on the way in which the message is perceived."[15] Every biblical interpretation is perspectival or biased; there is no single interpreter who is completely detached from his/her environment, experience and culture. No context, language or culture is superior when it comes to biblical interpretation. Unfortunately, the early missionaries made Africans believe that the Western culture was superior, and more acceptable to God than African culture. The missionaries came with the idea that everything African was unchristian and so an African had to be Europeanized before qualifying to be Christian. They erroneously assumed that their view on biblical interpretation is applicable to all contexts. The need to understand God and the Bible from the African perspective and culture and to break the

---

[14] Mojola, interview, 24/1/2019.
[15] Adamo, "Decolonizing African Biblical Studies", 4.

hegemony and ideological monopoly that Western biblical scholars have long enjoyed both serve as justification for ABS.

Thirdly, ABS is a prerequisite tool for African Christian theology. For centuries, theological discourses have been dominated by Western ideas. Westerners formulated theology, and Africans read Western-formulated theology. Since Western theologizing does not seriously take into consideration the existential issues crying for attention in Africa, there is the need for Africans to formulate their own theologies based on Scripture, the African worldview and realities, and church tradition. The task of doing African theology is not possible without first developing African hermeneutics. Gerald West underscores this point when he asserts that, "The separation of biblical studies from other theological disciplines, so common elsewhere, cannot be allowed to happen in African biblical studies."[16] African biblical hermeneutics therefore, forms the basis upon which an authentic African Christian theology could be developed.

Historical Development of African Biblical Studies

The developments that have characterized African Biblical interpretation can be classified into three phases, namely Reactive and Apologetic (1930 to the 1970s), first steps toward inculturation and Liberation (the 1970's to the 1990s), and inculturation hermeneutics and contextual Bible study (from the 1990s onwards).[17] We shall proceed to outline each of these stages briefly.

Reactive and Apologetic Stage (1930-1970s)

The first stage in the development of African biblical studies is the reactive and apologetic stage (1930-1970s). The approach of this first stage was a reaction to the early missionary approach used by Western missionaries in Africa. R.S Sugirtharajah[18] listed and discussed various ways by which colonization of biblical interpretation took place in the missionary era. The first mark of colonization of biblical interpretation is Inculcation, that is, "the use of the Bible as a vehicle for inculcating European manners." Here, local customs and worldview were labeled as barbaric while Western ones were considered Christian. Missionaries attributed the socio-economic progress of the Western society to the society's acceptance of the Christian faith.

---

[16] Gerald West, 'On the Eve of an African Biblical Studies: Trajectories and Trends', *JTSA* (1997) 99: 99-115:101.
[17] Ukpong, "Models and methods on Biblical interpretation in Africa", 81-289.
[18] R.S Sugirtharajah, *The Bible and the Third World:* Precolonial, Colonial and Postcolonial Encounters (Cambridge: Cambridge University Press, 2001), 61-73.

Encroachment, that is, "the introduction to the 'other' of alien values, under the guise of biblicization," in order to repudiate the local culture because of its perceived inability to serve as a channel for propagating the Christian faith, also marked missionary interpretation of Scripture. The local culture was considered as one which was theologically and conceptually impoverished needing to be "born again, baptized and Christianized" in order to make it a proper channel for transmitting Christian truths. Africans were given "Christian" names during baptism because it was assumed that their African names were not "holy" enough for a Christian to bear.

The third mark of the colonization of biblical interpretation is Displacement, that is, the displacement of local culture. This is the direct opposite of cultural encroachment. In societies where the missionaries found cultures full of egalitarian values, they considered it as "a hindrance to their understanding of the 'progressive' native of the gospel." These customs and values were regarded as undermining the viability of Christian virtues and the colonial project. They displaced these values by considering them as a sign of the people' primitiveness. Drumming, clapping and dancing which form a major part of the African religious life were silenced in favor of the quiet "dignity" of church organs, which accompanied foreign tunes and rhythms.

More so, analogies and implication, that is, the juxtaposition of biblical and secular history as a weapon against those who resisted colonial intervention, have played a major role in the colonial interpretation of the Bible. The Bible stories were read to justify the cruelty and suffering caused to Africans by violent invasion of the Europeans. Mofonkeng for example has observed that most young Blacks in South Africa "have categorically identified the Bible as an oppressive document by its very nature and to its very core" and hence demands "its expulsion from the oppressed Black community."[19] This happened because "these young Blacks, like many people in the formerly colonized countries, have experienced a situation, in their case under the white apartheid system, where the Bible was used as an instrument of domination and oppression."[20]

Besides, the textualization of the Word of God also marks colonial biblical interpretation. Textualization means the idea that no religious teaching was of any value except it is in written form. The missionaries erroneously assumed that oral cultures were empty and were waiting to be filled with written texts. By considering textuality as the ultimate measure of authentic religion, the

---

[19] Cited by Robert Aboagye-Mensah, *Dynamics of Preaching the Word: God Still Speaks* (Adwinsa Publication Ltd: Accra, 2011), 18.
[20] Aboagye-Mensah, *Dynamics of Preaching the Word*, 19.

missionaries discredited the oral tradition of the local people. The final mark of colonial interpretation is the Historicization of faith, that is, the affirmation of biblical religion as a historical faith, thereby regarding non-biblical religions as "pagan 'other' of Christianity." Sacred texts of other religions were viewed as "mythological absurdities and amatory trifles" which have no historical or eschatological significance.

As a reaction to this kind of approach to mission, Africans adopted a comparative approach that compares the Bible text, language, religion and culture with African text, language, religion and culture,[21] and the possible physical contact between Africa and the ancient Hebrews.[22] This method was applied especially to Old Testament studies to bring out the relevance of African culture to the study of the Old Testament and the relevance of the Old Testament to Africa and Africans. Topics such as marriage, funeral, sacrifice, land, society, kinship and chieftaincy featured prominently in theological discourses of this period. The comparative methodology was criticized on the basis that Africa and ancient Israel are geographically apart. Ukpong however argues that since the comparative approach focuses only on existential (not essential) continuities and discontinuities between the two cultures its findings are valid.[23] This methodology did not however yield practical results that could inform Christian life and thought in the practical sense.[24]

First Steps Toward Inculturation and Liberation (1970s-1990s)

During the early post-colonial era (in the late 1960s and early 1970s), African scholars, having come to the conclusion that Western biblical exegesis was not suitable for Africa,[25] began to work toward a more pragmatic way of interpreting the Scriptures in order to deal adequately with the African worldview.[26] John S Mbiti traces the history of biblical studies in Africa to the 1966 "Consultation of African Theologians" in Ibadan, Nigeria.[27] This conference, which was hosted by Bolaji Idowu, the first Chair in the Study of

---

[21] Ukpong, "Models and methods on Biblical interpretation in Africa", 282-284.
[22] JJ Williams, *Hebrewisms of West Africa: From Nile to Niger with the Jews* (London: George Allen & Unwin, 1930).
[23] Ukpong, "Models and methods on Biblical interpretation in Africa", 282-283.
[24] Ukpong, "Models and methods on Biblical interpretation in Africa", 282-283.
[25] Clifton R. Clarke, "In our Mother Tongue: Vernacular Hermeneutics within African Initiated Christianity in Ghana," *Trinity Journal of Church and Theology* 15 (2005): 52-68.
[26] See George Ossom-Batsa, "African Interpretation of the Bible in Communicative Perspective," *Ghana Bulletin of Theology* 2 (2007): 91-104.
[27] Mbiti, J.S. *Bible and Theology in African Christianity* (Oxford: Oxford University Press, 1986), 73.

African Religions in Africa, (in 1969) yielded the publication of *Biblical Revelation and African Beliefs*, edited by Kwesi Dickson and Paul Ellingworth.

By the mid-1970s the reactive and apologetic model began to give way to a more practical and theological model that centers on the African context. Scholarly opinions organized themselves in two major ways of reading Scripture, namely the inculturation approach and liberation theology.[28] Inculturation refers to the process of adapting the interpretation and proclamation of the gospel message to different cultural settings. According to J. M. Willigo and others, it is the "honest and serious attempt to make Christ and His message of salvation evermore understood by people of every culture, locality and time." [29] This process assumes that the gospel message is dynamic and must be understood in accordance with the cultural settings of its recipients. Willigo and others state further that, inculturation involves "the reformulation of Christian life and doctrine into the very thought-patterns of each people.... It is the continuous endeavor to make Christianity truly 'feel at home' in the cultures of each people."[30] This process "aims at the mutual enrichment of cultures in the dynamic life of an individual and Christian community."[31]

Two main sub-categories are identifiable under the inculturation Hermeneutics, namely *Africa-Presence-in-the-Bible studies* and *evaluative studies*. The African-presence-in-the-Bible model focuses on the presence of the African continent and its people in the Bible and their contribution to the history of God's salvific plan for humankind.[32] Before this time European biblical scholarship, which dominated the world had either concealed African presence in the Bible or given no attention to it. Adamo asserts that throughout his education in Nigeria and the USA, he heard nothing about African presence in the Bible.[33] Adamo and most of his contemporaries had their postgraduate education outside Africa because most of the institutions in Africa (at that time, that is, between the 1960s and 70s) did not offer postgraduate programs in theology and religion.[34] Adamo's study reveals that

---

[28] Ukpong, "Developments in Biblical interpretation in Africa," 7.
[29] J. M. Waliggo et. al., *Inculturation: Its Meaning and Urgency* (Nairobi: St. Paul Publications Africa, 1986), 12.
[30] Waliggo et. al., *Inculturation*, 12.
[31] Joseph Okech Adhunga, Woman as Mother and Wife in the African Context of the Family in the Light of John Paul II's Anthropological and Theological Foundation: The Case Reflected within the Bantu and Nilotic Tribes of Kenya (Dissertation Catholic University of America, 2012), 427.
[32] Ukpong, "Models and methods on Biblical interpretation in Africa," 284-286.
[33] Adamo, "Decolonizing African Biblical Studies", 11.
[34] Adamo, "Decolonizing African Biblical Studies", 30.

there is no foreign nation and its people mentioned in the Bible more frequently than Africa and Africans, about 867 times.[35] The African presence in the Bible covers every literary genre. As we shall demonstrate soon, Africans contributed economically, religiously, militarily, socially, and politically toward the survival of ancient Israel.[36]

Mensah Otabil's *Beyond the Rivers of Ethiopia* gives us a very good example of this methodology. He believes that inferiority complex is one of the factors that makes Africans underdeveloped and so most of his readings of the Bible are geared toward empowering Africans and helping them to overcome inferiority complex. [37] In this book, Otabil corrects misconceptions that black people are cursed and hence not part of God's plan of salvation. He considers the Western perception that Africans are poor because we are descendants of Canaan who was cursed by Noah, as a means of holding back black people.[38] Otabil refers to Genesis 9:25 and contends that Africans are not cursed.[39] He argues (convincingly, we think) that God blessed Noah and his sons (9:1) and so Ham carries that blessing.[40] Noah was aware that since God had blessed Ham already he could not curse him; that is the reason why he imputed the curse unto Canaan, the yet to be born son of Ham (Gen. 9:25; see also Num. 23:30). Otabil traces the black race to Cush, the son of Ham, and contends that Cush was never cursed but received a double blessing as the first born (see Gen. 9:25 and 10:6).[41] He encourages Africans "to redefine our theology to establish the true liberty of Christ in the lives of our people (black people)." [42]

Otabil then makes a case for the presence and impact of black (African) personalities in God's salvific history for humankind. He cites a number of black people who played significant roles in God's plan in human history to push his argument further. For example, Moses, the person God used in delivering his people from Egypt, was brought up in Egypt and was well versed in Egyptian civilization (Acts 7:22). He had a black wife (Num. 12:2) who contributed to his successful leadership.[43] Jethro, Moses' father-in-law who was a black person, taught Moses some principles of management.

---

[35] Adamo, "Decolonizing African Biblical Studies", 30.
[36] Adamo, "Decolonizing African Biblical Studies", 30.
[37] Mensah Otabil, *Beyond the Rivers of Ethiopia: A Biblical Revelation on God's Purpose for the Black Race.* (Accra: Altar International, 1992).
[38] Otabil, *Beyond the Rivers of Ethiopia*, 16.
[39] Otabil, *Beyond the Rivers of Ethiopia*, 18.
[40] Otabil, *Beyond the Rivers of Ethiopia*, 18.
[41] Otabil, *Beyond the Rivers of Ethiopia*, 38.
[42] Otabil, *Beyond the Rivers of Ethiopia*, 19.
[43] Adamo, "Decolonizing African Biblical Studies", 32.

Otabil urges blacks to rediscover their inheritance which is linked to God's salvific history, and considering themselves as central to this plan, do away with any mindset that hinders their economic development.[44] It was a Cushite (a black person, an Ethiopian) Ebed-Melech who had "the moral courage to challenge the king of the princess' wrongdoing" when the prince had Jeremiah put in a dungeon (Jer. 38:7-13).[45] Also, Africa was a place of refuge for Abraham (Gen. 12), Joseph and Jacob (Gen. 41:45). In addition, when Jeroboam rebelled against his father, he took refuge in Africa (I King 11: 40). Most importantly, when Herod was looking for a way to kill infant Jesus, God instructed Joseph to escape with the child to Egypt (Matt. 2:13-19). In addition, Simon of Cyrene (in the Northern part of Africa) was a compassionate African, who helped Jesus to carry his cross, the symbol of salvation (Mark 15:21; Matt. 27:32; Luke 23:26). The Ethiopian eunuch was an African Finance Minister who got converted and brought Christianity to Africa (Acts 8:26-40). For Otabil, without liberation of the African mind, there can be no socio-economic development: "We have to break these mental barriers to development."[46] Based on this assumption, he challenges blacks to "take control of their own churches, and stop subscribing to white stereotypes of blacks."[47]

The evaluative approach to inculturation reading of the Bible, evaluates "the encounter between African religion, culture, and the Bible, and evaluates this encounter in terms of an African understanding of the Bible"[48] in order to facilitate the communication of the message of the Bible within the African context, from which a new understanding of Christianity can evolve that is both Christian and African.[49] Ukpong has identified at least five different approaches within the evaluative approach.[50] The first approach evaluates elements of African culture, religion, beliefs, concepts or practices (that have been ignored) in terms of the biblical text, in order to give it a Christian expression and practical application thereof. The second approach uses a biblical text or theme to challenge elements of African culture and religion while the third interprets a text against the background of African culture and religion, in order to give a new understanding of the text in an African setting. The fourth approach deals

---

[44] Otabil, *Beyond the Rivers of Ethiopia*,73.
[45] Adamo, "Decolonizing African Biblical Studies", 33.
[46] Otabil, *Beyond the Rivers of Ethiopia*, 72.
[47] Otabil, *Beyond the Rivers of Ethiopia*, 87.
[48] Ernest Van Eck, "The Word is life: African theology as Biblical and contextual theology," *HTS* 62 (2)2006: 679-701: 683.
[49] Ukpong, "Models and methods on Biblical interpretation in Africa," 286.
[50] Ukpong, "Developments in Biblical interpretation in Africa," 9-11.

with continuity between African culture and Christianity while the fifth is a study of biblical texts with the goal of identifying biblical models for aspects of contemporary church life and practice in Africa.

Apart from inculturation, liberation hermeneutics also emerged within this period. Liberation Theology (hermeneutics) is the outcome of attempts to unite theology and socio-political concerns of the society.[51] It is relevant to Africa because it addresses issues such as oppression, poverty, injustice and marginalization. Liberation theologians argue that Africans have been victimized by colonialism, imperialism, exploitation and oppression. Therefore, Liberation Hermeneutics uses Scripture "as a resource for struggle against oppression of any kind based on the biblical witness that God does not sanction oppression but rather always stands on the side of the oppressed to liberate them."[52] God's deliverance of Israel from Egypt (in the book of Exodus) is a key text for the hermeneutics of political liberation. Biblical texts such as Exodus 23:11 and Deuteronomy 15:1-11 (God's call of Israel to take special care of the poor amongst them), Amos 2:6-6 and 5:21-24 (God's call for social justice and Luke 4:18-19 and 6:20-21, 7:21-22 (Jesus' sympathetic attitude to and teachings in favor of the poor and sick) form the basis for hermeneutics of economic liberation. Liberation hermeneutics stresses the economic and political liberation of Africans and investigates how the Bible has been used as an instrument of oppression, power, domination, marginalization, and/or manipulation and how to liberate the victims.

Black and Feminist Hermeneutics are two major strands of Liberation Hermeneutics. Black Theology deals with issues of apartheid and racial discrimination that prevailed in South Africa until 1994.[53] Black Hermeneutics interprets the Bible in such a way as to address issues of spiritual, social, political, and economic oppression of blacks. In Black Hermeneutics, the experiences and struggles of blacks are therefore crucial. This method challenges the Euro-American interpretative framework on the basis that it tends to legitimize oppressive ideologies against Blacks.

Feminist Hermeneutics, on the other hand, is the result of the struggle for women's liberation. It addresses the liberation of women not only in contemporary society, but also in the life of the church. To liberate women, Feminist Hermeneutics exposes patriarchal structures (as well as other oppressive elements) within Bible texts as well as the legitimizing and

---

[51] Ukpong, "Developments in Biblical interpretation in Africa," 7.
[52] Ukpong, "Developments in Biblical interpretation in Africa", 12.
[53] Ukpong, "Developments in Biblical interpretation in Africa", 12

perpetuating of these interpretative structures by interpreters of the Bible. Therefore, Feminist Hermeneutics enables women to combine their life struggles with belief in Scripture by creating an egalitarian reading of the Bible, where men and women have different roles of equal importance in the application of the lessons of Scripture.

Inculturation Hermeneutics and Contextual Bible Study (from the 1990's onwards)

Modern inculturation Hermeneutics traces its origin to the late Justin S. Ukpong, a Nigerian New Testament scholar. In the view of Ukpong in inculturation, "the meaning of a text is a function of the interaction between the text in its context and the reader in their context."[54] Ukpong published an article in 1996 to introduce this method into scholarly circles.[55] According to Ukpong "inculturation hermeneutics is a contextual hermeneutic methodology that seeks to make any community of ordinary people and their social-cultural context the subject of interpretation of the Bible through the use of the conceptual frame of reference of the people and the involvement of the ordinary people in the interpretation process."[56] Ukpong's approach to hermeneutics regards the history of the biblical text not as an end in itself, but as a means to an end. In other words, inculturation Hermeneutics focuses on making the Christian message relevant to the African religio-cultural context.[57] Ukpong thus argues, "Thus in inculturation hermeneutics, the past collapses into the present, and exegesis fuses with hermeneutics."[58] For Ukpong, "inculturation Biblical hermeneutic" drives the application of the inculturation paradigm to biblical interpretation.[59] Inculturation biblical interpretation seeks to read the biblical text from the present socio-cultural perspectives without compromising the sacredness and authority of the Bible in ethical and

---

[54] Ukpong, "Developments in biblical interpretation in Africa: Historical and hermeneutical directions", in G.O. West & M.W. Dube (eds.), *Bible in Africa, Transactions, Trajectories and Trends* (2001) 11–28Leiden: Brill, at 24.
[55] Jean-Claude Loba-Mkole, "Rise of Intercultural Biblical Exegesis in Africa" *HTS* 64(3) 2008 1347-1364 at 1347.
[56] Ukpong 2002, 12; italics author's emphasis.
[57] Ukpong, "Developments in Biblical interpretation in Africa", 7.
[58] Ukpong "Inculturation Hermeneutics: An African Approach to Biblical Interpretation" in D. Walter & L. Ulrich (eds.), *The Bible in a World Context: An Experiment in Contextual Hermeneutics* (Grand Rapids, MI: William B. Eerdmans, 2002), 17-32.
[59] Ukpong, "The Parable of the Shrewd Manager (LK 16:1-13): An Essay in the Intercultural Biblical Hermeneutic" *Semeia* 73 (1996): 189-210.

theological formulation.⁶⁰ In inculturation hermeneutics the African social-cultural context is central to the interpretive process. Thus according to Ukpong '… the African context forms the *subject* of interpretation of the Bible. The grid through which the Bible is read is developed from within Africa herself …'⁶¹ Obviously, this approach has very little to do with the Western hermeneutical framework. Inculturation hermeneutics has two major tasks. The first task is the appraisal of the cultural-human dimension of the Bible with respect to its cultural settings. The second task is to appropriate the message of the Bible in today's context.

According to Madipoane Masenya the following characteristics of inculturation may be delineated.⁶² Firstly, inculturation emphasizes the role of the reader's context in interpretation. In this process, the African social-cultural setting is to be intentionally made the subject in our interpretive endeavors. In Ukpong's view, "… the primacy of the reading activity is located not among individual theologians working in isolation but among theologians working among communities of ordinary people – it is the ordinary people that are accorded the epistemological privilege."⁶³ The Bible is considered as the record of the experiences of ordinary people expressed in stories, prayers, songs and other means. Therefore, the ordinary people must be given epistemological privilege.

Secondly, for Ukpong, the Bible is a key resource in inculturation hermeneutics. Like any other hermeneutical approach, inculturation hermeneutics involves an engagement with the biblical text in order to decipher contemporary significance for today's readers. The text of the Bible has the capacity to effect both personal and societal transformation required for socio-economic development in the lives of African Christians.

Third, for Ukpong, exegesis and hermeneutics are not to be considered as separate entities. Though exegesis searches for the meaning of a text in its original context, it is not an end in itself. Once the meaning of a text in its

---

⁶⁰ Jean-Claude Loba-Mkole, "Rise of Intercultural Biblical Exegesis in Africa" *HTS* 64(3) 2008 1347-1364 at 1350.
⁶¹ Ukpong, "Developments in Biblical Interpretation in Africa: Historical and Hermeneutical Directions," G.O. West & M.W. Dube (eds.), *Bible in Africa, Transactions, Trajectories and Trends* (Leiden: Brill, 2001), 11-28.
⁶² Madipoane Masenya, "Ruminating on J. S. Ukpong's Inculturation Hermeneutics and its Implications for the Study of African Biblical Hermeneutics today" *HTS Teologiese Studies/Theological Studies* (2016): 1-6.
⁶³ Ukpong, "Inculturation hermeneutics", 20.

original context is determined, there is the need to show its relevance for the contemporary society; unless this is done the outcome of exegesis is useless.

A key challenge associated with ABS is the diversity in the culture/worldview of Africans. The diverse worldviews held by Africans make it difficult to develop a unified African context. In spite of this difficulty, Ukpong[64] has outlined common areas that must underline African worldview:

   i. Worldview of a unified cosmos—no distinction between the physical and the spiritual.
   ii. Divine origin of the universe—A Creator God is central in African religion as in the Bible.
   iii. The important role of 'communality' in defining both individuals and society.
   iv. Emphasis on 'concrete' rather than 'theoretical'.
   v. Recognition of the supernatural as 'a given' in African cosmology.
   vi. Direct relevance of the interpretation to the community as a primary question of the interpretive process.

Contextualization is the process by which the gospel is translated into a culture in a way that makes the people understand and respond to it in their own socio-cultural setting. Contextual Bible Study assumes that the reading of Scripture is contextually informed. In other words, the context within which one is reading the Bible plays a role in his/her understanding of the biblical text. The focus of contextual Bible Study is to let people hear God speak to their own context. This involves both trained readers, that is those who have received biblical training and from who ordinary readers can learn, and ordinary readers, that is those who read the Bible in an untrained or pre-critical manner. The critical readers have something to offer the church and the community and at the same time have something to learn from the ordinary readers. Critical reading implies reading the Bible in its historical and sociological context without ignoring its literary form. Both the trained reader and the untrained reader are expected to read the Bible in an individually and socially transformative manner. Contextual Bible Study should be such that both trained and untrained readers read together rather than the trained reader reading for the ordinary reader.

---

[64] Ukpong, "Rereading the Bible with African eyes: Inculturation and Hermeneutics", *JTSA* 41 (1995): 3-14: 9-10.

African Biblical Studies

The following steps may be used to construct contextual Bible Study.

i. Identify an issue to be contextualized, for example, naming ceremony, chieftaincy, marriage, funeral or conflict.

ii. Collect adequate information about the prevailing practice within the community.

iii. Select biblical text(s) related to the cultural practice, bearing in mind the needs of the untrained reader.

iv. Select the mode of reading and study questions.

v. Select the response/application.

vi. Appraise the existing practice in the light of the studies conducted so far.

vii. Formulate and discuss how the practice could be given a Christian expression in the community.

The Four-legged-stool Hermeneutical Model

In her book *African Hermeneutics,* Elizabeth Mburu discusses a number of ways by which Africans can make meaning out of the Bible with their own cultural framework. We find her four-legged-stool hermeneutical model as a suitable model for the African context and so we have decided to summarize her thought for our readers.[65] The four-legged-stool hermeneutical model proposes that African hermeneutics must involve four major players which form the legs of the four-legged stool (shown in figure 1 below). The seat of the stool constitutes the application of the text and it is supported by the legs.

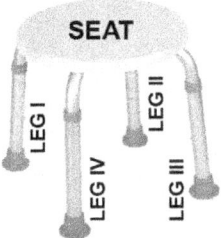

Fig. 7.1. The four-legged-stool hermeneutical model.

---

[65] Most of what follows come from Elizabeth Mburu, *African Hermeneutics* (Carlisle: HippoBooks, 2019), 65-89.

Leg 1: Parallels to the African worldview

The first leg of the hermeneutical stool has to do with parallels to the African context. The African must begin the hermeneutical process by "identifying the theological and cultural contexts that are the primary contributors to our own worldview, as well as relevant features of social, political and geographical contexts."[66] This leg, in addition to helping the African to start from a familiar position in his or her search for meaning, also helps him or her to identify areas of discontinuity between the African context and the biblical context.[67] This means that part of our context can help us understand the text and yet, another part may hinder our understanding. It is important to note that the biblical worldview must always prevail when it contradicts our own worldview. Thus, the biblical worldview must be used as a lens through which our African world is viewed, not the other way around. Giving priority to the biblical worldview helps to check syncretism.

The first leg is an appreciation of the contribution of the reader's world to the understanding of the text. The biblical text is then to be seen as a narrative piece which may always facilitate an interaction between the world of the narrator and that of the audience (today's readers). The areas of common interests are crucial in achieving this interaction. When the African reads about bareness of Sarah or Hannah (1 Sam. 1-2) he or she can easily picture the trauma these women would have gone through in their society. These stories can facilitate our understanding of the Bible as Africans. However, there are other stories that contradict the African worldview. For example, the story of the rich man and Lazarus after death though tells us that the spirit of humans lives after death in accordance with the African worldview, also tells us that the African concept of reincarnation is unbiblical. When this happens, the reader is expected to use the biblical idea to correct his or her unbiblical assumption.

Leg 2: Theological Context

The theological context comes next. This leg has to do with the theological emphasis of the biblical text in its literary context. In the Western hermeneutical framework, theological emphasis may not come at this point. In the African context however, people would normally consider theological context before historico-cultural contexts. The religious nature of Africans accounts for this observation. Africans, being notoriously religious, would

---

[66] Mburu, *African Hermeneutics*, 67.
[67] Mburu, *African Hermeneutics*, 67.

normally like to know what a text says about God and their everyday life realities before asking about the history behind the text.

At this point some applications of the text may begin to run through the reader's mind. Such applications must be confirmed later in the hermeneutical process. Therefore, they must not be considered as final at this point. The theological context involves the interactions between two horizons, namely, the biblical context and the reader's context. The interaction is based on the assumption that the meaning of a text to its original audience is similar to its meaning to the contemporary reader. A text cannot mean to a reader what it did not mean to its first audience.

Theological deductions from a text are informed by the similarities and differences drawn from the first leg. Deductions from the second leg must however not dictate how the other legs are understood. Mburu notes, "while our interpretation must not contradict the theology expressed through the text, our assumptions about the theology of specific texts or of an entire book must not be allowed to dictate our interpretation without consideration of the other contexts. A holistic approach is advisable."[68]

Leg 3: Literary Context

The third leg deals with the literary genre of the passage under consideration. Each biblical passage belongs to a particular genre.[69] Humans use specific genres to communicate specific kinds of information; the Bible in a similar way employs different genres depending on the message to be transmitted. Identifying the kind of genre is crucial in determining how to interpret the text. The way a narrative is interpreted is quite different from how poetry is interpreted. Clues from everyday life can help in the interpretation at this point. For example, African daily life is full of proverbial statements and so the African can easily appreciate the book of Proverbs. A book like Ruth can also be understood easily as an African story. The fact is that literary genre determines the hermeneutical principle to be adopted. Just as there are rules for every game, so are there rules for interpreting each genre. Some of the things that the reader needs to pay attention to include literary techniques, language, and literary flow. At this point, the initial conclusions made from the first two steps are to be confirmed or modified based on findings from this stage.

---

[68] Mburu, *African Hermeneutics*, 72.
[69] The various literary genres are covered in chapter five and the reader is advised to find out more from that chapter.

Leg 4: Historical and Cultural Context

The fourth leg of the hermeneutical stool has to do with the historical, economic and cultural settings that gave rise to the text.[70] Every biblical text emerged from a historico-cultural context; that context needs to be considered. In the historical-critical method developed by Westerners, an understanding of the historical context is sought before later considering what theological ideas are found in the text. However, as noted earlier, for the African, the theological import of the text is usually sought before the historical analysis. The historical and cultural contexts are to help the read shape deductions made when working on the first three legs. Mburu summarizes the fourth leg in the following words: "The fourth leg of the hermeneutical stool involves recognizing that the Bible cannot be understood in isolation from its historical and cultural contexts. A crucial aim of our study of the Bible is to understand what the text meant in its original context. To do so, we must enter into the world of the author and allow that world to guide our understanding."[71]

Seat: Application

The purpose of applying the four steps outlines above is to arrive at the right application. The application of a text refers to the significance of the text to the contemporary reader. The reader needs an answer to the question: "What must I do?" The answer to this question is what is referred to as the application of the text. All the four legs must be in contact with the seat and support it. Therefore, an application that is not supported by the legs is invalid.

Earlier we stated that some applications may go through the reader's mind as he or she goes through the legs. The final step, the seat, is expected to validate the tentative applications that the reader had, going through the other steps. Mburu points out that "Given the holistic African approach, application should be understood to be taking place subconsciously from the point we first begin to engage with the text. Indeed, the text should bring up not just a mental or emotional response but also a practical one"[72] This means that the last step is just a confirmation of how the text is expected to inform our lives.

The meaning of the text is usually one, which is the author's intended meaning (or authorial intent). However, the application can be many. The meaning must come before any application can be deduced. The distinction

---

[70] Details of contextual analysis are found in chapter three of the study.
[71] Mburu, *African Hermeneutics*, 84.
[72] Mburu, *African Hermeneutics*, 84.

between the meaning and significance of a text is evident in African folktale. After telling the story the meaning becomes evident and the narrator tells the listeners the lessons that can be derived from the story. In applying the meaning of the text to the African context one has to "Distinguish between the trans-contextual content of Christianity and its attendant forms and expressions in African culture", "disengage the trans-contextual or non-cultural doctrines of Christianity from the biblical cultural forms" and "reframe these trans-contextual truths in African cultural forms and expressions."[73] In other words, the reader has to determine which practices in the text are culture-bound and which ones are not, then reframe those that are cross-cultural into his or her context. The command to honor one's parents has trans-contextual significance. However, what a child should do as a sign of honoring his or her parents may differ from context to context. One has to consider how this should apply to a given context.

Conclusion

ABS, reads the Bible from an African perspective to address peculiar concerns of Africa. ABS has developed in three major stages since the 1930s. The first stage has been reactive and apologetic, the second stage is one of inculturation and liberation and the third stage is inculturation hermeneutics and contextual Bible Study. Over-reliance on the West for theological training, lack of support for research, lack of access to current journals and books, incompetent scholars in the field of biblical studies are some of the challenges facing African Biblical Studies today. Going forward, institutions of higher learning in Africa must make it part of their mandate to promote African biblical scholarship. Churches may sponsor pastors/members to pursue biblical studies so that they can contribute their quota to church life.

Review Exercise

1. What is inculturation? How has it developed over the past few decades?

2. How does the existence of diverse cultures pose a challenge to African biblical scholarship? How are we to deal with this problem?

3. Carefully explain the expression African Bible Studies.

---

[73] Mburu, *African Hermeneutics*, 87-88.

4. With relevant examples, explain what is meant by African presence in the Bible.

5. What is Liberation Hermeneutics? How relevant is it to post-colonial Africa?

6. What are the major contributions of J. S. Ukpong to the development of ABS?

7. How different is inculturation Hermeneutics from Liberation Hermeneutics?

8. What are some of the main differences between Western Biblical Hermeneutics and African Biblical Hermeneutics?

9. Is it necessary to have a unique way by which Africans interpret Scriptures? Explain your answer.

Chapter 8

Mother-Tongue Biblical Hermeneutics

Language is the hall-mark and the most enduring artifact of any society. It plays significant roles in social interaction and transmission of religious and socio-cultural values across cultures and generations. The demand to theologize in one's mother-tongue was pointed out by Nelson Mandela in his assertion, "If you talk to a man in a language he understands, that goes to his head. If you talk to him in his language, that goes to his heart."[1] Like Mandela, we believe that mother-tongue Scriptures and hermeneutical principles are effective tools for making people speak with God in their own language, to integrate the Christian and cultural identities. The present chapter discusses issues related to this developing method of Biblical Hermeneutics.

Some Key Contributors to Mother-Tongue Biblical Studies in Ghana/Africa

One of the foremost Ghanaian scholars who advocated the use of mother tongue in Christian discourse is the late Professor Emeritus Kwesi Abotsia Dickson (1929–2005). As a pioneer in African Christian theology, he emphasized the role of culture in the everyday theological discourse, hence his advocacy for contextual theology through relevant curriculum. His zeal for African theology and African-brewed hermeneutics made him design a course titled: *Old Testament, African Life and Thought* which he taught at the University of Ghana for many years. He argued that, "The [Christian] faith can be meaningful only when Christ is encountered as speaking and acting authentically, when he is heard in the African languages, when culture shapes the human voice that answers the voice of Christ."[2]

Dickson showed exceptional concern for the foundational role of the Bible and an appropriate translation of scripture in the life of the Church, especially in the Church's teaching ministry. He argued that a thorough study of the mother tongue was a channel through which Scripture could be owned by the African Christian. Dickson argued that the acceptance of other concepts as possible ways of God's self-revelation to humankind is a foundational truth

---

[1] "Mandela in his own words," CNN homepage, June 26, 2008, accessed April 9,2018 from http://edition.cnn.com/2008/world/africa/06/24/mandela.quotes
[2] Dickson, as cited by Ekem Inaugural Lecture, 161.

that must be established even before one attempts to do Theology in Africa.³ Therefore, before the introduction of missionary concept of God, Africans already knew and worshipped God. In the process of contextualizing the Christian message, it must be acknowledged that cultures differ in their conception of God and life, and this may require forms of expression and understanding peculiar to a given culture or people.

From Dickson's viewpoint, doing African Christian Theology requires the use of African concepts and understanding of the Religions to guide one's comprehension in the adoption of the Western Christian input. Dickson, therefore, argued that "The African approach to the Bible cannot but take account of the fact (that) there is much in common between the religio-cultural background of the Bible and African life and thought."⁴ His point is well understood if one considers various ways in which Africans demonstrated belief in God before the advent of missionary Christianity. Names of cultural symbols (eg. *Gye Nyame*, except God), pouring libation to the Supreme Being, use of God's name in proverbs and songs were some of the means through which African pre-missionary-Christian faith was expressed. According to Dickson the Eucharist in which we commemorate the sacrificial death of Christ and share a common meal is comparable to sharing the mutton or beef of a sacrificed sheep or cow by Africans, which in the African setting symbolizes the sharing in the life of the victim as a means of enhancing the unity which binds the participants into one social unit.⁵ The African communal life system enhances their appreciation of the need to participate in the Eucharist. Hence, Christ, the sacrificial lamb who is to be shared in a common meal, is the basis of the unity and health of the African community.

Kwame Bediako also contributed immensely toward the development of mother tongue theology. On the importance of people's mother tongue in their apprehension of God, Bediako states, "The ability to hear in one's own language and to express in one's own language one's response to the message which one receives, must lie at the heart of all authentic religious encounters with the divine realm…"⁶ because "God speaks into the African context in African idioms, and that it is through hearing in African mother tongues 'the great things God has done' (Acts 2:11), that African theology emerges to edify not only

---

³ Kwesi A. Dickson, *Uncompleted Mission: Christianity and Exclusivism* (Mary Knoll, New York; Orbis Books, 1991), 110-123.
⁴ Dickson, *Uncompleted Mission*, 110 – 123.
⁵ Dickson, *Uncompleted Mission*, 123.
⁶ Kwame Bediako, *Christianity in Africa: The Renewal of Non-Western Religion* (Maryknoll, New York: Orbis Books, 1995), 60.

the African church but the church world-wide."⁷ The point is that Africans must not only use Bibles translated into their mother tongues but must also theologize in their vernacular. The explosion of Christianity in Africa in the 21st century is largely due to the availability of vernacular Bibles. "Language itself becomes then," says Bediako "not merely a social or psychological phenomenon, but a theological one as well. Though every human language has its limitations in this connection, yet it is through language and for each person, it is through their mother tongue that the Spirit of God speaks to convey divine communication at its deepest to the human community."⁸

Another African scholar, Lamin Sanneh, argued that, "If Christ could be at home in Greek philosophy and thereby reinvigorate the ideas and values of a pagan order, there could be no bar to his performing a comparable role among other peoples in other times."⁹ Sanneh therefore says, "Success of Christianity will ultimately come to depend securely on its vernacular roots...Translation would consequently help bring us to new ways of viewing the world, commencing a process of revitalization that reaches into both the personal and cultural spheres."¹⁰ He believes that the remarkable growth of African Christianity in the 20th century is the fruit of African vernacular Bible translation. These vernacular translations of the Bible, Sanneh observes, adapt indigenous terms, concepts, customs and idioms for the central categories of Christianity in order to make the Christian message meaningful to the receiving community.¹¹

In recent times, the Very Rev. Prof. John David Kwamena Ekem has distinguished himself in the area of mother tongue theologizing/hermeneutics in Africa. According to Ekem, a person's mother-tongue differs from a vernacular in that the latter is the common language of a region or group; a person living in that region may not even be fluent in the vernacular.¹² One's mother tongue is the indigenous language, which identifies him/her or confirms and affirms who a person is, where he/she comes from and his/her

---

⁷ Bediako, *Jesus in Africa*, vii.

⁸ Bediako, *Christianity in Africa*, 60.

⁹ Lamin Sanneh (ed). *Translating the Message: The Missionary Impact on Culture* (Maryknoll, New York: Orbis, 2009), 61.

¹⁰ Sanneh, *Translating the Message*, 52-53.

¹¹ L Sanneh, "Gospel and Culture: Ramifying Effects of Scripture Translation," in Stine, P.C. ed., *Bible Translation and the Spread of the Church, The Last 200 Years* (Leiden: Brill, 1990), 16-17.

¹² John D. K. Ekem, "Jacobus Capitein's Translation of 'The Lord's Prayer' into Mfantse: An Example of Creative Mother Tongue Hermeneutics," *Ghana Bulletin of Theology* 2 (July 2007), 66-79, at 67.

sense of identity.[13] Ekem defines Mother Tongue Biblical Hermeneutics (MTBH) as the use of "viable tools for the scientific analysis of the phonetic, phonological, morpho-syntactical and semantic component" of a mother-tongue in the process of interpreting the Bible for the society.[14] In his Professorial Inaugural Lecture, the astute scholar set an eight-fold agenda for MTBH.[15]

i. Intensive study of the ancient biblical languages, namely, Hebrew/Aramaic and Greek;

ii. Preparation of context-sensitive Study Bibles in local Ghanaian/African languages.

iii. Introduction and development of Septuagint (LXX) Studies. Students will be offered the opportunity to explore this important document which traces its origins to Alexandria in Egypt and therefore emerges from an African context, and serves as vital transition to the New Testament.

iv. Introduction and development of Targum Studies, whereby students will be guided to critically examine the Aramaic foundations of some New Testament documents with particular reference to the Gospels.

v. Promotion of academic analysis of biblical texts in the various Ghanaian/African mother tongues, using the highest standards of biblical scholarship.

vi. Dramatization of biblical message as a logical sequel to its academic analysis.

vii. Use of the mother tongue to reflect, from a biblical perspective, on a relevant socioeconomic, religio-cultural and political issues confronting the communities today.

viii. Equipping people at the grassroots to arrive at an informed understanding of burning theological issues that confront the Church today.

---

[13] Ekem, "Jacobus Capitein's Translation of 'The Lord's Prayer'", 67.
[14] John D. K. Ekem, "Professorial Chair Inaugural Address," *Journal of Mother Tongue Biblical Hermeneutics* 1 (2015a): 158-74, at 166.
[15] Ekem, "Professorial Chair Inaugural Address," 164-165.

Ekem must be commended for setting the agenda for this developing area of study. We now put these agenda into three categories and offer brief discussions of each of them. We group agenda i, ii, iii, and iv under "the study of mother tongue and ancient biblical languages," agenda ii and v under "development of vernacular Bible study aids" and vi-vii under "innovation, creativity and relevance."

Elements of Mother-Tongue Biblical Studies

Study of Mother Tongue and Ancient Biblical Languages & Translations

The first principle is that participants in MTBH must have a working knowledge of ancient biblical languages, including Hebrew, Greek and Aramaic and ancient translations such as LXX and Targums, as well as their respective mother tongue languages. This is summed up in Ekem's assertion that MTBH "requires proficiency in one's own mother tongue, a comprehensive understating of the biblical world, mastery of the biblical languages, and thorough acquaintance with the worldviews of various African communities."[16] Knowledge about the biblical languages will enable the interpreter to have an "original" understanding of the biblical text. This will help him/her avoid the errors committed by Bible translators (of say the English Bible or even the mother tongue) on which most Africans rely for their theological formulation. Knowledge about these languages will go a long way to help Africans translate and interpret the biblical text more correctly.

Let us use Colossians 1:15 to illustrate how proficiency in biblical and mother languages can help us have a better translation and interpretation. The second part of the text describes Christ as *prototokos pases ktisis,* ("the firstborn of all creation," verse 15b NRSV). The Akan rendition is *adebo nyinaa abakan* (literally, the first to be created); *abakan* means first to be given birth to. The meaning of *abakan* within the Akan context leads to the theology that Jesus was the first to be created. This kind of theology is however not supported by the immediate context. There are other designations of Christ in the passage—for example, creator of all things (v. 16), sustainer of all things (v. 17) —that point to his priority and superiority over creation. Also, the firstborn (*prototokos*) created "all things" (v. 16) points to the fact that he cannot be part of creation. More support can be obtained from an examination of the Hebrew word *bekhor*. *Bekhor* comes from the b-k-r stem which stands for "first." Besides its use in a sense of "first to open the womb" or "first to be born", *bekhor* may be used in the

---

[16] Ekem, "Professorial Chair Inaugural Address," 166.

sense of having the greatest position, dignity, and honor (Esau - Gen. 25:29 ff; 49:3; 2 Chron. 21:3). It is the latter sense which dominates the Old Testament use of *bekor*. From all indications, the idea carried by *prototokos* is not that Christ was created but that he is the source of all things; he precedes all things and is the progenitor. With this understanding it is recommended that the Akan community looks for a better way of expressing this idea correctly. Our knowledge of the Akan language reveals that the Akan word *farebae* (meaning source) is a preferred Akan equivalence of the Greek word *prototokos*. Not only will the use of this word promote a better theology for the Akan community, it will also help readers to get a better understanding of their own language.[17]

The LXX and Targum cannot be left out of the agenda for MTBH. The LXX is the Greek version of the Hebrew Bible that originated from Alexandria (Egypt, in Africa), in about 260 BC when Jews in the Diaspora needed a Greek translation to facilitate the spread of the Sacred text because Greek had become the language of their everyday communication. The *Targum* refers to the Aramaic translation of the Hebrew Scriptures (the OT). The *targums* (or *targumim*) originated from the synagogue, where after reading the Hebrew text, the Aramaic version was also read and given Aramaic interpretation for the benefit of Jews who could no longer speak Hebrew. The *Targums* were often accompanied by interpretation from the scribes and hence they may be considered as forms of commentaries. By the second or third century BCE the Aramaic versions had replaced the Hebrew text in the synagogue. They were often paraphrased but sometimes literal too. *Targums* had glosses for the following functions: "(1) to resolve textual difficulties by interpreting obscure words or simplifying syntax, (2) to harmonize conflicting texts, (3) to reconcile the biblical text with accepted tradition, (4) to incorporate specifics of Pharisaic-rabbinic Judaism into the text, (5) to provide specificity to historical, juridical, or religious allusions, and (6) to either strengthen or mitigate the force of a scriptural passage."[18]

The *Targums* are not only useful in studying the Old Testament (because they give us ideas about how ancient Jews interpreted the Old Testament) but also for the study of the New Testament (especially the Gospels) because by the time of Christ Aramaic was the common language spoken in Israel. Some New Testament writers seem to have used targumic interpretation in the writings. For example, the statement "Vengeance is mine, I will repay" (Rom. 12:9; Heb.

---

[17] The 2018 Asante-Twi Bible renders *prototokos* as *farebae*. However, the Fante, and Akuapem versions have not done this.
[18] Bruce M. Metzger, *The Bible in Translation Ancient and English Versions* (Grand Rapids: Baker Academic, 2001), np (Pdf version).

10:30) which is a quotation from Deuteronomy 32:35 does not conform to the Hebraica (Hebrew text) or the LXX. Therefore, mother-tongue biblical scholars need to study these ancient translations to enhance their understanding.

The importance of mother tongue languages in ministerial formation cannot be overstated. European missionaries who introduced the Christian faith to Africa "realized rather thankfully that mother tongue Scriptures held the best prospects for the people's full appropriation of the faith."[19] They had to learn and speak the local language to enhance their task. In the same way, the pastor/minister is a missionary sent to a community whose language is critical in achieving his missionary goal. Ekem therefore, argues that "Pastors/Ministers in training should also be given an opportunity to do part of their formal theological studies in languages used by communities among whom they are going to minister."[20] This contention comes against the backdrop that in most African countries the languages of the colonial master (such as French, English and Portuguese) is the medium of instructions in seminaries and universities. Ekem is, therefore, calling attention to the need to replace these foreign languages with local ones so that the seminary graduate will be well equipped in their language with which they theologize in their ministry. Various institutions in Africa have centers for teaching Mother-Tongue Hermeneutics. In Ghana, the Trinity Theological Seminary, Legon, has a Center for Mother-Tongue Biblical Hermeneutics [CMTBH]; Akrofi-Christaller Institute also has a department for Mother-Tongue Hermeneutics. The CMTBH, of which Ekem is the director and the occupant of Kwesi Dickson-Gilbert Ansre professorial chair of Biblical Exegesis & Mother Tongue Hermeneutics, organizes short courses in Hebrew, Greek, Ga, Akan, and Ewe for pastors and others to enable them to have a working language in these languages, and hence improve upon their ministry. The center emphasizes the need to interpret the Bible using Ghanaian (African) languages and making the interpretation relevant for their context.

Ekem must be commended for such a policy which requires that ministers must be made to learn the language of the people they are to minister to as part of their ministerial training. However, there are some challenges that will hinder the realization of his dream in the near future.[21] Firstly, most of the local languages spoken in Africa have not been put into written form. Secondly, most

---

[19] Isaac Boaheng, Early Christian Mission in Ghana in *Rethinking the Great Commission*
[20] John D. K. Ekem, *Interpretation of "Scripture" in Some New Testament Documents: Lessons from the Ghanaian Context* (Accra: African Christian Press, 2015b), 20.
[21] The second and fourth points come from Daniel Nii Aboagye Aryeh, "Contemporary Hermeneutics: An Examination of Selected Works of John D. K. Ekem on Mother Tongue Biblical Hermeneutics for the African Context," *The Journal of Inductive Biblical Studies* 4/2:182-210 (Summer 2017):187.

theological materials available for study have been written in languages other than the African mother tongues. To address this second challenge, Ekem has been producing and urging others to develop context-sensitive study helps for mother-tongue theologizing. Thirdly, the diversity in languages in a country makes it difficult to have resources (personal and material) for using each of these languages as a medium of instruction. Fourthly, the frequent transfers of ministers from one community to another of a different mother tongue make it difficult to implement the suggested policy. While we call for a re-examination of the proposed policy based on the difficulties identified, we believe it is crucial that African theologians find ways of contributing their quota to the development of MTBH. Steps must be taken to address each of the difficulties mentioned above in order to reach the goal of using mother tongues for both ministerial formation and ministry proper.

Development of Mother Tongue Bible Study Aids

The second element in MTBH is the use of mother tongue Bible commentaries and Study Bible aids. Ekem contends that "The varied mother tongues of Africa have a lot to offer by way of biblical interpretation in Ghanaian/African languages as a viable material for interpretation, study Bibles and commentaries."[22] The most important Christian document to be produced in one's mother tongue is the Bible. However, the task of African Biblical scholars should not end at the publication of mother tongue Bibles. Mother tongue Bibles must be complemented by "local language Bible commentaries, local language Bible dictionaries and other study aids to facilitate effective interaction with Scriptures."[23] This does not however mean Ekem is underestimating the importance of commentaries and study aids in English and other major languages. Rather, his point is that these local materials are required to link the Bible to local African religious, cultural, and social values without having to go through a foreign language and culture. Ekem's view corroborates Bediako's assertion that, "the ability to hear in one's own language and to express in one's own language one's response to the message which one receives, must lie at the heart of all authentic religious encounters with the divine realm."[24]

---

[22] J. D. K Ekem, "Interpreting 'The Lord's Prayer in the Context of Ghanaian Mother-Tongue Hermeneutics" *Journal of African Christian Thought*, Vol. 10, No. 2, December 2007: 48-52: 47.
[23] Ekem, "Professorial Chair Inaugural Address," 166.
[24] Bediako as cited in Moses O. Biney, *From Africa to America: Religion and Adaptation among Ghanaian Immigrants in New York* (New York: New York University Press, 2011), 91. https://books.google.com.gh/books?id=tHETCgAAQBAJ&pg=PA91&lpg=PA91&dq

The fruits of the various campaigns for mother-tongue Scriptures and study aids yielded the publication of the *Bible in Africa* in 2000, *African Bible Commentary* in 2006 and *African Study Bible* (ASB) in 2016. These publications bring out the connection between Scripture and Africa's myriad cultures. John Jusu and Matthew Elliott therefore state that "Africa is quite a diverse continent, but there are similarities, common issues, and a shared cultural core that make Africans authentically African."[25] The content of the ASB was built around a framework designed by African leaders with the aim of enhancing Christian discipleship in the African context. Written by over 300 Africans, the ASB uses the African culture to enhance the reading and understanding of the biblical message. It includes about 500 African proverbs and culturally-relevant application notes.

Maxey has noted that "[S]ince we are dealing with a translatable faith and translated Scriptures, mother tongues, new languages, and the potential for new idioms become central and are crucial in opening up fresh insights into our understanding of the doctrine of Christ."[26] It can be added further, as Bediako observes that "God speaks into the African context in African idioms, and that it is through hearing in African mother tongues 'the great things God has done' (Acts 2:11), that African theology emerges to edify not only the African church but the church world-wide".[27]

Interpretive Creativity, Innovation and Relevance

The third element of MTBH is interpretive creativity and innovation. Gerald West (writing about two decades ago) also drew attention to the need for African biblical scholarship to arrive at a biblical interpretative framework that is quite distinct from what has been formulated by the west.[28] Such a hermeneutical framework, according to West, should not aim at rejecting the grammatical-historical and literary studies that, though dominant in western biblical studies also, serve as general principles that are relevant to ABS.[29] What African scholars

---

[25] John Jusu and Matthew Elliott "The Africa Study Bible: God's Word through African Eyes" *Reading the Bible in Context* Issue 2 (2016):4-7 at 5.

[26] James A. Maxey, *From Orality to Orality: A New Paradigm for Contextual Translation of the Bible* (Eugene: Cascade Books, 2009), 55. https://books.google.com.gh/books?id=dflLAwAAQBAJ&pg=PA55&lpg=PA55&dq

[27] Kwame Bediako, *Jesus in Africa: The Gospel in African History and Experience* (Akropong: Editions Clé and Regnum Africa, 2000), vii.

[28] Gerald West, "On the Eve of an African Biblical Studies: Trajectories and Trends," *JTSA* (1997) 99: 99-115:102.

[29] West, 'On the Eve of an African Biblical Studies: Trajectories and Trends', 102.

should do is to innovatively and creatively apply Scripture to address the African context in ways that interpreters from other perspectives may never do. This kind of creativity and innovation which both Ekem and West advocate for, can be seen in the contextual interpretation of Jesus's statement "You are the light of the world, and the salt of the earth" (Matt. 5:13) given below. Most commentaries from the western perspective explain that light directs our path and salt preserves and adds flavor. In Ghana (where the present writers come from) and many other places in Africa, this understanding may be meaningful because the context favors this understanding. However, reading this same text from the context of another part of Africa allows new insights to emerge. From the perspective of some people the text is more meaningful if both metaphors in the text are understood as relating to showing direction. John Susu, the General Editor of the *African Study Bible*, interacted with a theologian from the southern part of Africa who gave the following explanation:

> In my village, when there is drought, the monkeys know where there is water. But, they will not lead humans to that water. [They will only go to the water when no human being is following them]. So, the people will trap a monkey and tie it up. Then, they will feed it [with] salt. After a day or two, the monkey will become very thirsty. At this point, the humans will release the monkey. Then, the monkey will not care if the human beings are following it or not; it will make straight for the source of water in order to satisfy its thirst.[30]

Therefore, it is by the help of the salt that humans find direction to the source of water. The point therefore, is that Christianity must make people thirst for the living water. This touches not only on the missionary mandate of the Church but also on the need for Christians to live in such a way as to attract others who thirst and hunger for the living water and the bread of life to come to Christ. He stated, "If your Christianity does not make people thirsty for the water of life, then it is worth nothing."[31] This understanding is different from the understanding that the salt in the metaphor represents preservation and the addition of flavor. The two perspectives on the salt metaphor are valid in their respective contexts. Again, in some African cultures, Jesus's love for his disciples and humility could be understood better from the story which says Jesus ate with his disciples than the one in which he washed their feet because feet washing is not a culturally understood event in

---

[30] Jusu and Elliott "The Africa Study Bible", 4.
[31] Jusu and Elliott "The Africa Study Bible", 4.

that context. Clearly, words are understood in one context as one thing, in another place and context they might mean something very different.

Creativity and innovation can also be in the form of dramatization of Scripture texts, especially narratives. In the African setting where the illiteracy rate is high, dramatizing the Christian message will enhance memorization, as the drama keeps it fresh in people's minds. African churches may have to form drama groups who will constantly have some lessons in drama for the benefit of the Church. The drama together with the academic analysis of the text will go a long way to enrich African biblical scholarship. In addition, MTBH must be relevant to the issues bothering the society. It must therefore provide practical steps necessary to solve relevant socioeconomic, religio-cultural and political issues confronting the communities today. In so doing MTBH will equip local people to arrive at an informed understanding of burning theological issues that confront the Church today.

Methodology for Mother-Tongue Biblical Hermeneutics

In spite of the various scholarly efforts geared toward the development of MTBH, not much has been said about the methodology. J. E. T. Kuwornu-Adjaottor, a former student of Ekem, has published extensively in the area of MTBH. In his "African Biblical Hermeneutics: A Methodology for Mother Tongue Biblical Hermeneutics," Kuwornu-Adjaottor proposes a nine-step methodology for MTBH as follows:

i. Identify a biblical text which you think has been wrongly translated into your mother-tongue;

ii. Discuss why the translation is problematic in your culture.

iii. State the methodology you will use, and the proponents.

iv. Do a study (an exegesis) of the text, using Bible Study resources- Dictionaries, Commentaries, Encyclopedias, Word Study helps, etc.

v. Find out what scholars have said about the text, how they interpret it and reasons for their interpretations.

vi. Discuss the usage of the concept in your language/culture; interview indigenous speakers of your mother tongue for deeper insights into the concept you are researching. Use local terminologies in your writing and explain them in English.

vii. Compare the text in your mother tongue with other Ghanaian translations you can read and understand.

viii. Analyze the mother-tongue translations; what do they mean? How are the meanings of the text similar to that of the Hebrew/Greek? How are they different? What might have accounted for the differences in translation?

ix. Come out with a new translation of the text that fits into your culture.[32]

The methodology outlined above indicates that mother tongue biblical studies requires a multifaceted approach, comprising biblical studies, Bible translation studies and language studies (i.e. Hebrew, Aramaic and Greek and the mother tongue). Standing on the shoulders of both Ekem and Kuwornu-Adjaottor, we propose a five-fold methodology comprising: identification of the problem; exegetical study of text (or word study); comparative study of the mother-tongue translation of the text/word; the search for a culturally appropriate rendition and a proposal for appropriate mother-tongue translation. We shall use the translation of *talanton* (in Matt. 25:15) as a case study in our discussion below to explain each of these steps.

Identification of the problem

Mother-tongue Bible Translation (and subsequent interpretation), has brought in its wake numerous challenges, which various translation agencies continue to grapple with in their bid to give the best version possible to the people. Most of these challenges come as a result of cultural, time, social and economic gaps between the Bible world and ours. The translation of units of measurements (weights, currencies), proper names, cultural idioms and practices are among the areas which pose many problems to translators. Presently, there are many texts whose renditions in the various Ghanaian mother-tongues are problematic due to some of the challenges mentioned above. The first step in MTBH, therefore, is the identification of non-accurate translation of a word/phrase or sentence in a given mother tongue. Once a problematic passage has been identified the researcher needs to explain, in clear terms, what exactly the problem is. There is the need to discuss, from the context of the recipients, why the issue identified is problematic or inadequate in that culture.

Of particular interest to this study is the translation of *talanton* (Matt. 25:15) into Ghanaian mother tongues. Most Ghanaian languages have no exact words

---

[32] J. E. T Kuwornu-Adjaottor, "African Biblical Hermeneutics: A Methodology for Mother Tongue Biblical Hermeneutics," *E-Journal of Religious and Theological Studies* 2015 (vol 1) 1-24: 17-18.

for the term *talanton*. Translators are therefore tempted to transliterate it (or borrow the English expression) and consider it as a loan word. The result of this practice is the difficulty Ghanaian mother-tongue readers face in understanding the thought expressed in the passage. The Asante & Akuapem-Twi and Fante versions, for instance, by rendering *talanton* as *talente*, put their readers at the risk of considering it as "talents", "gifts" or "special abilities." The Ewe Bible (2010) translates it as *sikaga*, "gold money". Giving a monetary value to *talanton* is also problematic because studies about this term show that it is not possible to know the exact value of talent in our context. The use of a generic term is better than quoting specific values. This problem has prompted this study that purposes to bring out the meaning of *talanton* in its biblical setting and to offer suggestions as to how this cultural expression may be rendered in order to meet both the physical and spiritual needs of Ghanaian mother-tongue readers in their own socio-religio-cultural settings.

Exegetical Study of Text (or Word Study)

The next step is to conduct a well-researched study of the background of the problematic word or expression in order to gain adequate understanding of it in the original context. This is usually done through exegesis (which includes word study). Acquiring adequate understanding of the expression is the key to discovering how to transfer the concept into the receiving culture. The exegesis must reflect a dynamic encounter between the biblical culture and traditional African culture as both of them continue to exert a powerful impact on African Christians.

In the case of Matthew 25:15 a solution to the research problem requires an adequate understanding of the Greek term *talanton*. The plural of *talanton* is *talanta* which is an accusative plural neuter noun. It occurs in two parables in the NT, the first in the Parable of the Unmerciful Servant where: "...one man owes his master 10,000 talents (*talanta*) ... and another man owes the first a hundred denarii." (Matt. 18:24). The second time *talanton* appears, it occurs in Matthew 25:15 in the Parable of the Talents where both monetary terms (talent and denarii) occur several times. *Talanton* corresponds to the Hebrew *kikkār* and represents the largest unit of weight in the Bible. The Hebrew *kikkār*, probably of Mesopotamia origin, was the basic unit of weight among the ancient Hebrews. In Mesopotamia it was divided into sixty minas. In the sacred system of weights, the Talmudic talent was equal to 60 Talmudic minas.

Before its use in the Bible it was known by the same name in Ugaritic but was pronounced *kakaru*. The relation between the talent and the shekel is defined in Exodus 38:25-26. Here we are told that a half shekel was brought by each of 603,550 men and it amounted to 100 talents and 1,775 shekels. Thus, a talent was 3,000 shekels among the Hebrews. In Mesopotamia, from where this system might have originated, a talent was 3,600 shekels. Talent was a unit of weight used by many other ancient civilizations, such as the Egyptians, Greeks, and Romans. Homer knew about talent and described how Achilles gave a half-talent of gold to Antiochus as a prize.[33]

In the Greco-Roman world, the word *talanton* could refer to a measure of weight or a measure of money. As a measure of weight, *talanton* was the largest unit ranging from 28 to 36 kg, or 60 to 80 sixteen-ounce pounds. In monetary terms, *talanton* had a fluctuating value depending on the metal (or monetary system) involved—be it gold, silver or copper. The term was not used for any particular currency.[34] A *talanton* of silver valued about 6000 denarii[35] and a gold talent valued about thirty times that much. A denarii was worth a day's wage for a laborer.[36] It therefore follows that a *talanton* of silver will be worth the salary of 6,000 days' work, approximately sixteen and a half years. *Talanton* was a unit for calculating significant wealth, not a coin. Peter Schmidt's view is that "no coin with this name was ever created."[37]

The difficulty the translator encounters in translating this term has to do with the means by which to estimate the exact value of a *talanton* in modern currency. At least three problems are encountered in trying to quote its exact value.[38] Firstly, we do not know the exact weight of *talanton* in the Greco Roman world. The values we have are ranges of weights or money. Secondly, we do not know what kind of currency the talents referred to in this parable was. There is no scholarly consensus as to whether the master gave his servants gold, silver or copper talents. Thirdly, the effect of inflation on the value of our currency also affects the probability of accurately giving a value for *talanton*. That being the case, it would only be a guess work to quote any exact amount of money as the exact value of the *talanton* Jesus meant in this parable.

---

[33] Homer, *Delphi Complete Works of Homer* (Np: Delphi Classics, 2015), np. https://books.google.co.ke/books?id=L2cbAgAAQBAJ&pg=PT1812&lpg=PT1812&d

[34] Ben Chenoweth, "Identifying the Talents Contextual Clues for the Interpretation of The Parable of the Talents (Matthew 25:14-30)" in *Tyndale Bulletin* 56.1 (2005) 61-72.

[35] Michael Magill, *New Testament TransLine: A Literal Translation in Outline Format* (Eugene, Oregon: Wipf & Stock, 2002), 63.

[36] T. Adeyemo (ed.), *Africa Bible Commentary* (Grand Rapids: Zondervan, 2006), 1189.

[37] Peter Schmidt, *Biblical Measures and their Translation Notes on Translating Biblical Units of Length, Area, Capacity, Weight, Money and Time* (SIL International, 2014), 29.

[38] L. Morris, *The Gospel According to Matthew* (Grand Rapids: William B. Eerdmans Publishing Company, 2002), 627.

Comparative Study of Mother-tongue Translation of the Text/word

It is very important to study how the text under consideration has been translated in other mother-tongues which the researcher can read and understand. If it becomes necessary to study it in a language the researcher cannot read and/or understand someone with a working knowledge in the language may be asked to help. The comparative study aims at discovering how various cultures have transferred the biblical text into their context. In Ghana, the Akan languages including Bono, Asante, Akuapem and Fante have similar vocabulary, with slight differences in spelling and pronunciation. A comparative study in these languages will help the researcher to have a broader Akan perspective of the term. We can analyze the mother-tongue translations to ascertain the meaning of the text and how it has depicted certain nuances to the Hebrew/Greek text. The differences in translation and what might have accounted for such differences is also noted here.

For a better understanding we look at Matthew 25:14-15 in Akuapem Twi Bible, Asante Twi Bible, Fante Bible and Ewe Bible.

Asante-Twi (1964): *Na ɛte sɛ onipa bi a ɔretu kwan akɔ baabi, na ɔfrɛɛ ɔno ara nkoa na ɔde deɛ ɔwɔ hyɛɛ wɔn nsa. Na ɔmaa ɔbaako **talente** nnum, na ɔbaako mmienu, na ɔbaako nso biako, sɛdeɛ wɔn mu biara ahoɔden teɛ; na ɔtuu kwan.*

(It is like someone who was traveling to a certain place, and he called his own servants and handed over his possessions to them. And he gave to one of them five talents, another two talents, and another one talent, according to each person's strength; and he went on a journey).

Asante-Twi (2012): *Na ɛte sɛ onipa bi a ɔretu kwan akɔ baabi, na ɔfrɛɛ ɔno ara nkoa na ɔde deɛ ɔwɔ hyɛɛ wɔn nsa. Na ɔmaa ɔbaako **talente** nnum, na ɔbaako mmienu, na ɔbaako nso baako, sɛdeɛ wɔn mu biara ahoɔden teɛ; na ɔtuu kwan.*

(It is like someone who was traveling to a certain place, and he called his own servants and handed over his possessions to them. And he gave to one of them five talents, another two talents, and another one talent, according to each person's strength; and he went on a journey).

Akuapem-Twi (2012): *Na ɛte sɛ onipa bi a ɔretu kwan akɔ baabi, na ɔfrɛɛ n'ankasa ne nkoa na ɔde nea ɔwɔ hyɛɛ wɔn nsa. Na ɔmaa obiako **talente** anum, na obiako abien, na obiako nso biako, sɛnea wɔn mu biara ahoɔden te; na ɔtuu kwan.*

(It is like someone who was traveling to a certain place, and he called his own servants and handed over his possessions to them. And he gave to one of them five talents, another two talents, and another one talent, according to each person's strength; and he went on a journey).

Fante Bible (2008): *Na ɔtse dɛ nyimpa a ɔrodɔ mu akɔ beebi a ɔfrɛɛ no nkowaa, na ɔdze n'adze a ɔwɔ hyɛɛ hɔn nsa. Na ɔmaa baako* **talente** *enum, ɔbaako so ebien, na ɔbaako so kor, dɛ mbrɛ hɔn nyina hɔn tum tse, na ɔkɔree.*

(It is like person traveling to a far place, and he called his servants and handed over his possessions to them. And he gave one of them five talents, another person two talents, and another person one talent, according to each person's power; and he went on a journey).

Ewe Bible (2010): *Dzifofiaɖufea ɖi ŋutinya sia: 'Ŋutsu aɖe le nugbe yim. Eyɔ efe dɔlawo, eye wotsɔ efe nunɔamesiwo de wo si. Ena* **sikaga** *akpe atɔ ame ɖeka, ena akpe eve ame bubu, eye wòna akpe ɖeka ame etɔlia; wo dometɔ ɖe sia ɖe ɖe efe ŋutete nu, eye wodzo yi nua gbe.*

(The Kingdom of heaven is like this story. A certain man was traveling to a far place. He called his servants and handed over his possessions to them. He gave five thousand gold coins to one person; he gave two thousand to another, and gave one thousand to the third person, according to their abilities and then went on a journey).

The Search for a culturally appropriate rendition

An appropriate understanding of the text in the mother-tongues gives the researcher the opportunity to search for a culturally appropriate terminology or expression that can accurately transfer the message of the biblical author into the mother-tongue of the researcher. This search may involve interviewing people who are well versed in the language. Linguists, chiefs, traditional spokespersons of chiefs and other traditional leaders may be consulted to seek ideas.

The search for an Akan term for *talanton* yielded the term *dwetire* (Asante and Akuapem) or *dwetsir* (Fante), each term referring to an amount of money that is substantial to start a profitable business. In Akan marriage ceremony, it is the money given to the woman and to start a business with, once married.[39] If *dwetire* equals a talent, then five talents amount to *dwetire mmɔho num* (five times *dwetire*), two talents *dwetire mmɔho mmienu* (two times *dwetire*) and so on. The qualifier *mmɔho* (times) may however be omitted without changing the meaning of the text. We leave the translator to make the appropriate choice. What is crucial is the term *dwetire* or *dwetir*. The use of

---

[39] T. E. Kyei, "Marriage and Divorce Among the Asante: A study undertaken in the course of the Ashanti Social Survey (1945)" in *Cambridge African Monographs* 14 (African Studies Centre, 1992), 126. pdf

this term does not only carry a better idea of *talanton* in the Akan setting but also eliminates the tendency of thinking of *talanton* as special ability.

Another way of rendering the text could be to say the man gave the first "*ne sika mu abupɛn nnum*" (five parts of his wealth/money). This rendering, though better than what we find in the Akan Bibles now, has some challenges. Firstly, it does not carry the idea that the amount given to even the third person could start a business. Its emphasis is on the fact that the master divided his money into eight and gave it out in the ratio 5:2:1. Secondly, it has the tendencies of making readers think that the master divided all his money into eight and shared among his servants. However, from the text we do not know whether it was all his wealth that he distributed or not. What we know is that he gave his servants multiples of an amount that is substantial enough to start a profitable business.

A proposal for appropriate mother-tongue translation

The study comes to a climax at this stage where the researcher, based on the outcome of the previous steps, proposes a culturally accurate rendition for the text under study. There may be more than one way of expressing the idea. The researcher must however choose the most appropriate one and explain why he/she has made that choice. The study must conclude with implications of the proposed rendition on the theology of the recipients.

In the case of our example (Matt. 25:14-15), we propose the following translations for the mother-tongues we have dealt with.

Asante-Twi: *Na ɛte sɛ onipa bi a ɔretu kwan akɔ baabi, na ɔfrɛɛ ɔno ara nkoa na ɔde deɛ ɔwɔ hyɛɛ wɔn nsa. Na ɔmaa ɔbaako* **dwetire** *mmɔho nnum, na ɔbaako mmɔho mmienu, na ɔbaako nso baako, sɛdeɛ wɔn mu biara ahoɔden teɛ; na ɔtuu kwan.*

(It is like someone who was traveling to a certain place, and he called his own servants and handed over his possessions to them. And he gave to one of them five times a working capital, another two times, and another, one, according to each person's strength; and he went on a journey).

Akuapem-Twi: *Na ɛte sɛ onipa bi a ɔretu kwan akɔ baabi, na ɔfrɛɛ n'ankasa ne nkoa na ɔde nea ɔwɔ hyɛɛ wɔn nsa. Na ɔmaa obiako* **dwetire** *mmɔho anum, na obiako mmɔho abien, na obiako nso biako, sɛnea wɔn mu biara ahoɔden te; na ɔtuu kwan.*

(It is like someone who was traveling to a certain place, and he called his own servants and handed over his possessions to them. And he gave to one of them five times a working capital, another two times, and another, one, according to each person's strength; and he went on a journey).

Fante: *Na ɔtse dɛ nyimpa a ɔrodɔ mu akɔ beebi a ɔfrɛɛ no nkowaa, na ɔdze n'adze a ɔwɔ hyɛɛ hɔn nsa. Na ɔmaa baako* **dwetir** *mmɔho enum, ɔbaako so mmɔho ebien, na ɔbaako so kor, dɛ mbrɛ hɔn nyina hɔn tum tse, na ɔkɔree.*

(It is like someone who was traveling to a certain place, and he called his own servants and handed over his possessions to them. And he gave to one of them five times a working capital, another two times, and another, one, according to each person's strength; and he went on a journey).

Ewe Bible (2010): *Dzifofiaɖufea ɖi ŋutinya sia: 'Ŋutsu aɖe le nugbe yim. Eyɔ efe dɔlawo, eye wotsɔ efe nunɔamesiwo de wo si. Ena* **asitsaga** *tefe atɔ ame ɖeka, ena tefe eve ame bubu, eye wòna tefe ɖeka ame etɔlia; wo dometɔ ɖe sia ɖe ɖe efe ŋutete nu, eye wodzo yi nua gbe.*

(The Kingdom of heaven is like a man traveling to a distant place. He called his servants and distributed his possessions to them. He gave one person five times the trading capital, to another he gave two times and to the third person he gave one unit of the trading capital, in accordance with each person's ability and went on the journey).

The word *asitsaga* employed in the Ewe rendering cannot be restricted to the vocabulary of marriage, showing how differently Akan and Ewe function as mother-tongues.

Conclusion

At the heart of the Christian message is the fact that God respects and speaks every language and wants to communicate to every individual in his/her heart language. The importance of mother-tongue Scriptures, MTBH and mother-tongue theologizing cannot be overstated. This study encourages African theologians to help develop this discipline. To theologize effectively in the mother tongue one needs an adequate understanding of the biblical world, especially cultural issues, as well as the world of one's mother tongue. Various resources are available for one to consult in dealing with difficulties in their work to enhance their understanding of cultural issues and hence determine how to appropriately transfer the thought to their people without distortions and ambiguities. This will reduce ambiguities in mother tongue theologizing/hermeneutics that result from obscure translations.

Review Exercise

1. Attempt a mother-tongue hermeneutical reading of Roman 1:1, clearly bringing out Paul's concept of ministry. How does this concept compare with contemporary Christian ministry in Ghana?

2. Examine the translation of three biblical idioms in your mother-tongue Bible, bringing out issues that you feel were not adequately dealt with.

3. Attempt a mother-tongue exegesis of Roman 5:12-21. What Christology can be derived from your exegesis? How relevant is the Christology derived from your study to African Christianity?

4. Translate John 1:1 into English and then into your mother tongue. Attempt an exegesis of the text and deduce the Christology of this text.

5. The Fante Bible translates *antichristos* as antiChrist while the Akuapem and Asante Bibles render the same term as anti-Kristo (cf. 1 John 1:18, 22). In your opinion what theological challenge can these translations pose to mother-tongue readers? How can we deal with these challenges?

6. Examine the translation of *prototokos* (Col. 1:15) in your mother tongue. How does the translation support or refute the theology that Christ is the first creature of God?

7. Discuss the methodology of doing MTBH in Ghana and illustrate each step with an example from your mother tongue.

8. Should we continue to translate the Bible into the various mother-tongues? Explain your answer with particular reference to the Ghanaian context.

9. Attempt a mother-tongue commentary on the Matthean Beatitudes.

10. What are the three key elements of African Biblical Hermeneutics?

11. Write an essay for or against the assertion that "African mother-tongue translations must start with the Old Testament and not the New Testament."

12. What exegetical insight can you derive from Genesis 22:1-11 when it is read from the perspective of your ethnic group?

13. To what extent do you agree with the view that, "Without foreign missionaries, mother-tongue translation would not have been possible"?

14. The Asante and Akuapem Bibles translate the expression νέφος μαρτύρων as *adansefoo mununkum* (clouds of witness) (Heb. 12:1). To what extent do you agree that the phrase should be rendered "*adansefoo bebiree*?"

15. Attempt an exegesis of Genesis 2:15. What lessons can we learn from your study in relation to environmental stewardship?

16. Does God require human sacrifice? Answer this question through an exegetical study of Genesis 22:1-11.

17. What creation story have you heard from your community? How does it compare and contrast with the creation account of Genesis 1? How should the insight drawn inform your community's attitude toward the environment?

18. Prepare a brief mother-tongue commentary on Romans 3:21-31.

Chapter 9

Women and Church Leadership in Africa: Exegetical Insights from two Pauline Texts

The issues of women leadership in the African Church is a contentious one because of the deeply entrenched patriarchal and hierarchical nature of most African societies. More often than not most interpreters translate biblical texts related to the issue through the lenses of gender roles in African society and culture. However, the present authors are of the view that a holistic understanding of the overall teaching of the Bible regarding Christian ministry will grant women the opportunity to perform every ministerial role in any capacity that the Holy Spirit calls them to work. In a brief chapter like the present one, one cannot offer a detailed study of all texts related to the subject matter. What we offer here therefore is a representation of what we believe the Bible teaches about female and church ministry.

Two Guiding Hermeneutical Principles

Often when people discuss the role of women in Christian ministry, with particular reference to Christian leadership, they make reference to two key texts, namely, 1 Corinthians 14: 34-35 and 1Timothy 3:1-7. From these texts they deduce that the Bible bars women from Christian leadership. To be sure, there are certain categories of Christian leadership roles that people do not dispute, a woman leading and teaching other Christian women, or a woman serving as a deaconess in church. More specifically, people tend to oppose the leadership of women over men and women. Some further reject female ordination in particular based on their interpretation of the above-mentioned texts.

These texts are famous for silencing women in the church and disconfirming other passages in the Bible that seem to support women leadership in the Christian Church. However, these texts must be fairly interpreted. The subject of women in Christian leadership must be examined holistically and dispassionately. The discussion ought to involve the entire biblical data on the subject beyond the two texts. While the focus of this chapter is on how not to use these two texts, conclusions reached will also be based on insights from many other Bible texts related to the subject.

Additionally, the two texts must be understood within the right cultural, historical and literary contexts. In this regard, the role of the context in determining the meaning of the content of a Bible text cannot be overestimated. To understand the intent of a biblical author, we must first determine the context of the writing. There is the need to distinguish what is culturally binding from what is cross-cultural and timeless. There is the need to appreciate the reason(s) that prompted what a biblical writer wrote. Understanding the intent of the text is a significant step in deciphering what it means and then applying it appropriately to one's context.

Another hermeneutical truth that helps in the proper understanding of a biblical text is the principle of interpreting Scripture in the light of Scripture. It is biblically unwarranted, hermeneutically inappropriate and theologically suicidal to treat texts in isolation from others. To be sure, treating texts in isolation leads to disfigurement, twisting and distortion of the intents of biblical authors. These initial thoughts would guide our exegetical comments on the two selected passages.

1 Corinthians 14:34-35 and Women Speaking in Church

The text reads "the women should keep silence in the churches. For they are not permitted to speak, but should be subordinate, as even the law says. If there is anything they desire to know, let them ask their husbands at home. For it is shameful for a woman to speak in church" (1 Cor. 14:34-35 RSV). Gordon Fee beautifully structures the text as follows:

The rule: The women must be silent in the churches.

The reasons: For

    a. It is not permitted for them to speak.

    b. But let them be in submission, even as the Law says.

The provision: If they wish to learn, let them ask their husbands at home.

The reason: For

    a. It is shameful for a woman to speak in the assembly.[1]

The same Greek word *gune* (translated "women) may mean "wife" or "woman."[2] There is therefore a debate regarding what Paul actually means by

---

[1] Gordon D. Fee, *The First Epistle to the Corinthians* (Grand Rapids, MI: Willaim B. Eerdmans Publishing House, 1987), 706.

use of *gune*. Does he refer to any woman (as it is the case in 1 Cor. 11:3-11 where it appears 11 times in the generic sense) or wives (as it is in 5:1; 9:5; 7:34)? Two contextual reasons suggest that Paul has married women in mind.[3] The idea of submission (*hypotassesthōsan*) when used in the New Testament in connection with women connotes married women who are to be subject to their husbands (cf. Eph. 5:22; Col. 3:18; Tit. 2:5; 1 Pet. 3:1, 5). The expression "their own husbands" (v. 35) also indicates that Paul has married women in mind. From the foregoing the present writers strongly believe that rather than using *gune* in the general sense, Paul uses it in the narrow sense to refer to married women alone. Thus, Paul's directive to women was made in the context of prohibiting a wife from critiquing her husband's message, since such an exercise was disgraceful.[4] One can agree with Lowery that Paul "wanted silence on the parts of married women whose husbands were present in the assembly, but he permitted the participation of other women when properly adorned (1 Cor. 11:2-6). Such silence would express their subordinate (but not inferior) relationship to their husbands."[5]

It should also be noted that the context of this text shows that Paul was addressing the issue of orderly worship, with particular reference to the use of spiritual gifts in the worship service. Paul clearly states in verse 34 that women should remain silent in the church. What is this supposed to mean? Elsewhere in chapter 11 of the same epistle where Paul was addressing proper dressing and behavior at Christian worship, he notes that a woman praying or prophesying in church ought to cover her hair (11:1-6). This implies that women were permitted to speak in Pauline churches because no one can pray and prophesy in church without speaking. The obvious question is: Can the same author permit women to pray and prophesy in church (chapter 11) while at the same time telling them to be silent in worship (chapter 14)? The seeming contradiction can be resolved only if proper attention is paid to the context of each of the imperatives.

---

[2] Paul Ellingworth and Howard A. Hatton, *UBS Handbook Series: A Handbook on Paul's First Letter to the Corinthians*, Second Edition (New York: United Bible Society, 1994), np. (electronic version)
[3] David K. Lowery, "1 Corinthians" in *The Bible Knowledge Commentary* (Colorado: David C. Cook, 1983), 541.
[4] E.E Ellis, "The silenced wives of Corinth (1 Cor. 14:34-35)", *In New Testament Textual criticism, its significance for exegesis: Essays in Honour of Bruce M. Metzger* (Oxford: Clarendon Press, 1981), 15.
[5] Lowery, "1 Corinthians", 541.

If 1 Corinthian 14:34 is interpreted superficially, by simply pointing to the initial impression it makes on the reader without recourse to the context, the result will be to make women invisible in church. This is even more so in Africa where the average congregation reports about 60% female membership. Some have argued that 1 Corinthians 14:34-35 constitutes an interpolation because it does not fit into the flow of thought of the overall argument of chapter 14. This is noted but even if the section is to stand in the text as legitimate, one is still faced with the challenge of the apparent inconsistency in the injunction to pray and prophesy in church with heads covered and to remain silent in church. Therefore, the expression "they are not allowed to speak" and "it is shameful for a woman to speak in the church" have a limited application (34-35).[6]

If we were to argue that the two imperatives can hold together, it would mean that women could participate in missionary work, proclaim the gospel to friends and family, pray in private and/or even embark upon evangelistic preaching in the open but when they go to church their liberty to proclaim the good news comes to an end. Besides, the context of verse 34-35 begins with verse 26. This verse suggests a charismatic community of worshippers possibly with no leaders and so people are led by the Spirit to do one thing or the other with no one authorized to regulate the service. Evidently, this mode of worship in the Corinthian church is entirely different from most contemporary worship services. When they met the believers were encouraged to contribute to the service in a form of hymn or praise, instruction and so on. This approach to worship had apparently resulted in confusion on occasion and so Paul is urging the believers to do everything orderly. He indicates that the best way to do this is to ensure that each activity is carried out with the right motive–that is, for the edification of the church.

Paul's concern was for the worship to be orderly. In this regard, women were not the only ones asked to be silent. Those speaking in tongues during the service are to be silent if there is no interpreter (14:28). If a prophet is speaking and a revelation comes to another, the first is asked to be silent (14:30). In verse 32, the prophets were asked to be submissive to each other based on the understanding that God is not the author of confusion. The last part of verse 33 ("...as in all the congregation of the saints") should be read with the rest of the 33 rather than adding it to the verse 34 as some translations do.

---

[6] F. F. Bruce, *New Century Bible* (New York: Harper Collins Distribution Services, 1971), 67.

1 Timothy 2:12-15 is often read with 1 Corinthians 14:34-35 to further exclude women from leadership in church, especially when it comes to playing roles during corporate worship. In 1 Timothy 2:12-15, the context suggests that the author was concerned about the controversies in the church. To deal with the controversies Timothy was sent to the church in Ephesus (1Tim. 1: 3). In verse 8, Timothy was told to "admonish men to pray with holy hands lifted, without anger and quarrelling." Regarding the women, the author's interest was about behaviors and attitudes that could disrupt the worship. To avoid such a situation, he asked women to learn in quietness and in submission. The author's intent for sending Timothy to Ephesus was to address the false teachings and heresies in the church (cf Rev. 2: 2) and other knowledge and myths that had led many astray. Most victims and targets of these false teachers were women (2 Tim. 3: 6) and like Eve, they were being deceived (1 Tim. 2: 14). The author's injunction to the women was a strategy for dealing with the deception of the women by the false teachers rather than forbidding women from teaching or speaking in church. Here too, Paul's reference is to married women. We reason this way because verse 15 cannot apply to unmarried women. Furthermore, 1Timothy 5 treats a number of problems caused by women (idleness, gossip, busy-bodies, saying things they ought not to) in connection with the false teachers. More so, the noun *hesychia* in 1 Timothy 2:11-12 means "quietness", that is "the absence of disorder" while the word *sigao* in 1 Corinthians 14:34 means "remain silent."[7] Lastly, it is important to note that the passage is regulating how women should learn just as all disciples should and not prohibiting them from teaching.

1 Timothy 3:1-7 and Women in Christian Leadership

The point has been made that some interpreters forbid female ordination on the basis of their interpretation of 1 Timothy 3:1-7. For some, the last phrase of verse one as the KJV renders it, "If a man desires the office of a bishop, he desireth a good work" further strengthens their argument. However, the Greek pronoun "*tis*" refers to either male or female. Therefore, using "anyone" or "whoever" instead of "a man" is a better translation. The passage itself is descriptive rather than prescriptive. The author wrote the epistle to address leadership issues in the church of Ephesus. Here, the author may as well be addressing a question which Timothy may have asked concerning a particular man (male person in a patriarchal context) who desired to be a bishop. It may be argued further that the requirement of an overseer to "be the husband of one wife" (v. 2) excludes women from ministry since a woman cannot be a

---

[7] Lowery, "1 Corinthians", 541.

"husband of one wife". In recognition of this difficulty the NRSV renders the phrase "married only once". In any event, if one were to hold the view that "be the husband of one wife" is the appropriate translation in context, then Paul, in whose name the epistle stands, would have been disqualified, since we have no evidence that he ever married. Besides, the text says nothing about the unmarried person desiring to be a bishop.

The author comes across as referring to the qualifications of a male person who desires to hold the position of a bishop in the church. This can hardly mean that the author was making statements that are intended for universal application for he was clearly addressing a local, pressing issue, and in a patriarchal context too. Therefore, this passage cannot be legitimately used to prevent women from being excluded from ordained ministry.

Women in Leadership the Community of God's People

The controversy surrounding women in Christian leadership is largely a New Testament discussion but there are texts in the Old Testament that offer very helpful insights into the discussion that should not be ignored. In Genesis 1:26- 28, God created male and female in God's image and after God's likeness. They were both given dominion over the earth. In biblical times, women were usually not educated in formal schools and rabbis were warned against teaching the law to women. Women who were considered respected did not take part in public life. Respected women were those who stayed within the confines of their homes. However, God uses all regardless of their gender to fulfil God's purpose and for God's glory. This is evident both in the Old Testament and in the New Testament.

Women in Leadership in the Old Testament

Women played various roles in ancient Israel's worship. Some were allowed to work in the tabernacle. Some were singers in the worship community. Others were prophetesses and judges who led God's people. Some even acted as war leaders. In Exodus 38:8, women were ministering at the gate of the tent of meeting. They could also become Nazirites (Numbers 6:1-2) and given a direct opportunity to serve the Lord. God selected both men and women to serve as prophets in Israel. The Old Testament mentions at least four prophetesses namely: Miriam (Exodus 15:20), Huldah (2 Kings 22:14-20), Deborah (Judges 4:4-16) and Noadiah (Nehemiah 6:14; perhaps a false prophetess). However, God uses whomever God chooses for God's purpose and glory.

Women in Leadership in the New Testament

Jesus had many women disciples. Women are described as having traveled with Jesus from Galilee to Jerusalem (Mark 15:40-41). At the empty tomb, in Luke 24: 1-8 two men in clothing that gleamed like lightning asked the women if they remembered what Jesus told them in Galilee about how the "Son of man must be delivered into the hands of sinful men, be crucified and on the third day be raised again". (v.7). In Luke 9:18-22, we find that Jesus was praying in private with his disciples with him when he gave the prediction about his death and resurrection.

Even though we have no evidence that the women disciples were there when Jesus made this prediction, one finds it curious that the angels would now ask the women if they remember what Jesus said in private to his disciples. Were the women there? Even if they were not present at the prediction, it is clear that the women would have known about the teachings of Jesus regarding his own death and resurrection which is why the angels felt duty bound to remind the women of this significant lesson.

After the resurrection, women were the first to whom Jesus appeared and the first to be commissioned to proclaim the good news of the resurrection. They were to proclaim the resurrection to the apostles (Matt. 28:9-10). Generally, disciples refer to all of Jesus' followers. However, women were not always mentioned in the Gospels even when they were present. Again, Paul's greeting in Romans 16:7 "Greet Andronicus and Junias "…they are outstanding among the apostles….." points to a further role of women in the early church. Junias is the only female named in the New Testament as an apostle. In the same chapter Paul mentioned women who were serving in leadership roles in the church. Phoebe (v. 1) was a minister or a deacon of the church in Cenchrea. Priscilla (v. 3, Acts 18: 18, 26) and Mary (v. 6) were leaders too. In Acts 2, as Peter preaches to the crowd to explain what was happening, he proclaimed that it was the fulfilment of Joel's prophecy: "And afterwards, I will pour my Spirit on people. Your sons and daughters will prophesy, your young men will see visions. Even on my servants, both men and women, I will pour out my Spirit" (Joel 2:28-29). Obviously, women were present at Pentecost and participated in the fulfillment of Joel's prophecy mentioned earlier. The ministry of the four daughters of Philip is another example of the ministry of the Holy Spirit through women as prophetesses (Acts 21: 9).

Moreover, Philippians 2:2-3 mentions two women; Euodia and Syntyche who had struggled along with Paul and other fellow workers. It is clear in 1 Corinthians 11 also that women were prophesying and praying in the church. Therefore, we cannot argue that women were allowed to prophesy and pray in the church but are not allowed to preach or teach or lead the church. If they prophesied in church then they also instructed people because prophecies instruct people as well (1 Cor. 14: 31). Speaking about the unity of believers in Christ, Paul writes in his epistle to the Galatians "There is neither Jew nor Greek, slave nor free, male nor female, for you are all one in Christ Jesus." (Gal. 3: 26-28). In ancient times before Christ, Gentiles and women did not have the privilege of studying or being taught the Torah and being part of the covenant society. Daily, Jewish males thanked and praised God that they were not born Gentiles, women or slaves. This is the prayer: "Blessed are you, Hashem, King of the universe, for not having made me a Gentile."[8] Blessed are you, Hashem, King of the universe, for not having made me a slave."[9] "Blessed are you, Hashem, King of the universe, for not having made me a woman."[10] The word *Hashem* derives from the Hebrew words—"*ha*" and "*shem*" which means "the" and "name" respectively. Therefore, *Hashem* means the name, in reference to YHWH. This Jewish notion is completed opposed by the New Testament. In the Post-resurrection era, every believer is baptized by the Spirit and clothed with Christ, we have become equal spiritually. The ancient differences no longer apply to the body of Christ. Hence we may all study the Bible, receive the gifts of the Holy Spirit and serve in the body of Christ as ministers or leaders or in whichever position the Lord calls us to.

The Limiting Role of Women in Africa

In patriarchal societies like those of Africa, women are generally expected to play supporting roles to men because the man is expected to play the dominant and the leading role. The typical African woman is expected to take care of domestic tasks. The roles are so deeply entrenched in African family systems that the woman is expected to constrain herself and live in conformity with these traditional expectations. Because of the dynamism of culture, in recent times, these expectations are gradually changing due to exposure to western cultures and education.

However, the perception and expectations of an ideal African woman has not changed. Patriarchal societies still promote male dominance and female subordination. It is seen as legitimate for men to be the authoritative figures with dominant power. The Akan of Ghana have strict traditional roles for women. Therefore, a woman who is assertive is often referred to as "ɔbaa akokɔnin" (literally, a woman cock). Another Akan saying, *ɔbaa to tuo a etwere*

---

[8] Chaya Diane Hager, *From Bogota to Madrid to Jerusalem: A Family's Fascinating Journey* (Brookline: Israel Book Shop, 2006), 51.
[9] Hager, *From Bogota to Madrid to Jerusalem*, 51.
[10] Hager, *From Bogota to Madrid to Jerusalem*, 51.

beema dane mu (when a woman buys a gun it is a man who keeps it for her), *baa tɔno nyadoa na ɔntɔno atuduro* (A woman sells garden eggs and not gun powder) also promotes male dominance over females. According to Diabah and Amfo, women are stereotypically perceived to pay special attention to their physical appearance, which is perhaps the fulfilment of their role as "sex object." Women are the focus of the man's sexual desires. This is sometimes reflected in the Akan proverb *ɔbaa kɔ adwareɛ na ɔkyerɛ a na ɔreyɛ ne ho yie* (If a woman goes to the bathroom and keeps long then she is dressing up). They further claim that women are dependent financially and emotionally on men.

The woman is absorbed in domestic activities and is therefore dependent on the man for almost everything. It is not surprising that a man boasts and takes the credit for his wife's beauty and achievements. The woman is considered not capable of her own achievements and her advancement is often ascribed to a husband if she is married or to her father or brothers or some other man if she is not married. Again, women are seen as naïve and defenseless or weak. The Akan perceive that the woman can easily be lured or deceived and therefore valuables cannot be entrusted to her. She is perceived as powerless, vulnerable and an opportunist who is only interested in herself and what she will get from a man. This is reflected in the Akan proverb *ɔbaa te sɛ ohuriiɛ; ɔnom mogya na ɔmma mogya* (A woman is like the tsetse fly; she drinks blood but she doesn't give blood).

Moreover, in much of African folklore, the woman is often portrayed as gossip, greedy, evil, disobedient and wicked, murderous (of husbands), ungrateful, cheating, lazy and apathetic. There is a very popular Akan folktale entitled "Why the Hawk (*Akorɔma*) Catches Chicks" In the story, the Hen (*Akokɔ*) does not contribute to the making of a drum, yet she hides and plays the drum in the absence of her friend (the Hawk), who is the owner. The story shows Mother Hen suffers serious punishment when her chicks get killed by Hawk always because she was a cheating, lazy and apathetic woman. She faces the condemnation of losing her offspring to the Hawk, ceaselessly. This was the agreement between the Mother Hen and her friend, the Hawk. She is the cause of the pain and anguish that her family will have to endure forever. In this folktale the woman is portrayed as lazy and apathetic and is always or mostly the cause of the problems or challenges in the family and society.

These ideas are from proverbs and folktale but, we should not lose sight of the fact that a lot is learned from them. It is worrying that if a folktale of this nature is told a young teenage boy, he grows up with the perception that women are witches, wicked, greedy, lazy and so on which affects his attitude and behavior toward women in a negative way. Again, these proverbs which are part of African speech, directly or indirectly reinforce the already existing stereotypical, negative and disrespectful view of women. If there is an effective corrective to the rhetoric just narrated, it should come from the Bible, the word of the God who loves and is just to everyone, male and female. If the Bible is thus interpreted to reinforce the African stereotype of women and the validation of patriarchy, then we have a huge problem on our hands.

Conclusion: Responsible Exegesis for Contextual African Theologizing

African Christianity has a duty to change these stereotypes against African women through responsible exegesis. When the core message of the Bible rather than the culture through which the message is mediated gets promoted there will be better integration between people's lives and Bible texts. If African theologians commit themselves to the faithful interpretation of the Bible, paying adequate attention to contextual matters their theologies will be life-affirming to the African communities which they serve. If, however, theologising in Africa is kept within the ambit of impressionism and the use of the Bible to promote personal ambitions and reinforce traditional patriarchal notions against women, the African Church faces the danger of future disintegration and ultimate annihilation as happened to the seven churches of Asia Minor listed in Revelation 2-3.

Review Exercise

1. How are females regarded in your society in relation to their male counterpart?

2. In what sense is male dominance affecting the development of females in your area?

3. In 1 Corinthians 14:34-35, was Paul subscribing to hierarchical views on gender relations, making men superior to women?

4. Can women be ordained? Explain your answer.

5. Discuss the role women played in the ministry of Jesus and state what lessons the African society can learn from this.

6. "Africa's traditional society was not always fair to women." Discuss.

Concluding Remarks

The study set out to develop an exegetical approach by which African Christians can understand and apply Scripture passages to their lives. The eight-chapter study devoted the first six chapters to discussing conventional methods of exegesis based on the Western worldview. The last two chapters focused on African Biblical Studies and African Mother-Tongue Biblical Hermeneutics. If by reading this book, one is better equipped to interpret and apply the word of God to his/her life, our purpose of writing this book would have been achieved. In this section we note and outline some of the major conclusions and implications of the study for African Christians. We acknowledge the relevance of conventional approaches like the historical-critical method, social-scientific approach and the like in deriving the message carried by a scriptural text. The importance of discovering the original meaning of a text before applying it to a contemporary situation cannot be over-emphasized. A text cannot mean to the contemporary reader what it did not mean to the original reader(s). Yet, these approaches should not be regarded as completely suitable for all contexts. They emerged from particular contexts and are most suitable for those contexts. That does not mean these conventional approaches have no role to play in African exegesis. In our candid opinion, Africans can use the conventional approaches in discovering the intended meaning of a biblical author and after that, derive applications based on the African worldview. Issues such as abject poverty, hunger, ethnic tensions, child abuse, corrupt leadership, war, terrible illnesses and other unpleasant realities must be at the center of African exegetical discourse. That is to say, African biblical exegesis must concern itself to link the biblical text with the realities of African contexts.

The exegetical approach we consider African involves four elements that interact, including, the text, the context of the text, the reading community, and the context of the reading community. The principle is stated as follows: The meaning of a text is obtained through the process of a community in a particular *socio-cultural context* reading *it* in relation to its *socio-historical context*. In the process, there must be an encounter between the contemporary socio-cultural context and the socio-historical context of the biblical text. There is the need to interpret a text from the perspective of the modern reader without isolating it from the original context. Priority is however, given to the context of the readers, which informs the questions the readers put to the text. The ethical demands of the Gospels including, love of

God and neighbor, respect for one another, justice, peace, inclusiveness and the like constitute a plumb line for checking the validity of such readings.

African Academic institutions have a huge role to play in developing and popularizing African readings of the Bible. In view of this, we implore various academic institutions in Africa to develop and teach courses that promote African ways of reading the Bible. Aside courses such as Old Testament and Africa Life and Thought, and Theologizing in African Languages which are taught in some institutions, others such as African Biblical Exegesis, African Presence in the Bible, and others should be developed by scholars whose scholarship relate to these areas. This study could be a beginning point in developing African Biblical Exegesis. The course African Presence in the Bible should aim at bringing to the fore the role of Africa and Africans in God's salvific history. Not only will this course deal with any kind of inferiority complex that results from the thought that Africans have no place in God's salvific history, it will also help democratize biblical exegesis in Africa. In all these, the academy must make it clear to everyone that African readings of the Bible are (explicitly) perspectival just as readings from other contexts are. As such there is no need to claim universality for any reading of the Bible. Similar contexts read the Bible similarly, while dissimilar contexts read it differently.

Further still, we may conclude that our limitedness as humans makes us incapable of appropriating every aspect of a text, no matter how hard we try. The implication of this fact is that even within the African continent or within the same country or among scholars, different aspects of a text may be more prominent than others. If so, then one should be careful how he/she judges other people's understanding of Scripture. This fact should however, not lead one into thinking that any interpretation of Scripture is acceptable. Whatever message one derives from the Bible must not contradict what God has revealed plainly in the Bible.

African Bible reading must prioritize the participation of the ordinary/ common people; that is non-elite. In Africa a lot of the people lack formal education; therefore, depriving them of the chance to read with other people will go a long way to stagnate church growth. The African Church must help the ordinary people to read through literacy programs. Bible study aids of local contents should also be developed and taught. The interpretations of ordinary readers could then be noted and developed to enhance a better understanding of the word of God. In the process, trained readers should not control the reading process or seek to "teach" what they already know as the meaning of the text. Rather, they must read as part of the community, and facilitate an interactive process that promotes critical thinking and sound understanding of the text. This collaborative reading process has the potential of helping readers to not only to understand the Bible based on their experiences (with God) but also helps readers to recognize and affirm the personal worth of others. This approach will also enable academic readers to access the rich resources of popular readings of the Bible which in turn will inform their scholarship.

A brief study of this kind cannot deal with all issues related to the subject matter. We therefore wish to end the study with suggestions for further research. One area that needs to be studied is the issue of mother-tongue Scriptures. Our experience in the work of translation has shown the need for a collaborative effort to revise most of our mother-tongue Bibles to give a better representation of the source text. Some of the most difficult areas for mother-tongue translators include the translation of cultural idioms, proper names (places, peoples), units of measures (weights, length, heights), figurative language (metaphor, simile) and poetic literature. We believe that a study on these areas will go a long way to enhance African Biblical Studies. More so, an empirical study of the use of mother tongue Scriptures in major African communities will go a long way to help develop African Biblical exegesis, and hence African Christian Theology. It is our strong conviction that further research in these and other areas will not only supplement our efforts but will go a long way in promoting African Biblical Studies.

Bibliography

Aboagye-Mensah, Robert. *Dynamics of Preaching the Word: God Still Speaks* (Adwinsa Publication Ltd: Accra, 2011.

Adamo, David Tuesday. "African Cultural Hermeneutics," *Vernacular Hermeneutics*, ed. Sugirtharajah. Sheffield: Sheffield Academic Press, 1999.

Adamo, David Tuesday. "Decolonizing African Biblical Studies" Professorial Inaugural Lecture delivered at the Delta State University, Abraka.

Adamo, David Tuesday. *Exploration in African Biblical Studies*. Eugene, Oregon: WIPF & Stock Publishers, 2001.

Adeyemo, T. (ed.), *Africa Bible Commentary*. Grand Rapids: Zondervan, 2006.

Adhunga, Joseph Okech. *Woman as Mother and Wife in the African Context of the Family in the Light of John Paul II's Anthropological and Theological Foundation: The Case Reflected within the Bantu and Nilotic Tribes of Kenya*. Dissertation Catholic University of America, 2012.

Amevenku, Frederick M. and Boaheng, Isaac. "Analysis of Law and Gospel in God's Salvific Plan" in *E-Journal of Religious and Theological Studies* 2(1): 2016, 188-212.

Amevenku, Frederick Mawusi and Boaheng, Isaac. "Reconciling saving faith and works of the law in Paul and James" in *Ghana Journal of Religion and Theology*, Vol. 7 (1) 2017: 66-80.

Aryeh, Daniel Nii Aboagye. "Contemporary Hermeneutics: An Examination of Selected Works of John D. K. Ekem on Mother Tongue Biblical Hermeneutics for the African Context," *The Journal of Inductive Biblical Studies* 4/2:182-210 (Summer 2017).

Augustine. *On Christian Doctrine*, translated by D. W. Robertson. New York: The Liberal Arts Press 1958.

Bayes, Jimmy D. "Five-fold Ministry: A Social and Cultural Texture Analysis of Ephesians 4:11-16" in *Journal of Biblical Perspectives in Leadership* 3(1) (2010):113-122.

Bediako, Kwame. *Christianity in Africa: The Renewal of Non-Western Religion*. Maryknoll, New York: Orbis Books, 1995.

Bediako, Kwame. *Jesus in Africa: The Gospel in African History and Experience*. Akropong: Editions Clé and Regnum Africa, 2000.

Biney, Moses O. *From Africa to America: Religion and Adaptation among Ghanaian Immigrants in New York*. New York: New York University Press, 2011.

Blomberg, Craig L. and Markley, Jennifer Foutz. *A Handbook of New Testament Exegesis*. Grand Rapids, MI: Baker Academic, 2010.

Bruce, F. F. *New Century Bible*. New York: Harper Collins Distribution Services, 1971.

Bruce, F. F. *The Gospel of John*. Grand Rapids, MI: Wm. B. Eerdmans, 1983.

Chenoweth, Ben. "Identifying the Talents Contextual Clues for the Interpretation of The Parable of the Talents (Matthew 25:14-30)" in *Tyndale Bulletin* 56.1 (2005) 61-72.

Clarke, Clifton R. "In our Mother Tongue: Vernacular Hermeneutics within African Initiated Christianity in Ghana," *Trinity Journal of Church and Theology* 15 (2005): 52-68.

Corley, Bruce, Lemke, Steve W. and Lovejoy, Grant I. *Biblical Hermeneutics*, second edition. Tennessee: Broadman Publishers, 2002.

Dickson, Kwesi A. *Uncompleted Mission: Christianity and Exclusivism*. Mary Knoll, New York; Orbis Books, 1991.

Duvall, J. Scott and Hays, J. Daniel. *Grasping God's Word*, 2d ed. Grand Rapids: Zondervan, 2005.

Ekem, J. D. K. "Interpreting 'The Lord's Prayer in the Context of Ghanaian Mother-Tongue Hermeneutics" *Journal of African Christian Thought*, Vol. 10, No. 2, December 2007: 48-52.

Ekem, John D. K. "Jacobus Capitein's Translation of 'The Lord's Prayer' into Mfantse: An Example of Creative Mother Tongue Hermeneutics," *Ghana Bulletin of Theology* 2 (July 2007), 66-79.

Ekem, John D. K. *Interpretation of "Scripture" in Some New Testament Documents: Lessons from the Ghanaian Context*. Accra: African Christian Press, 2015b.

Ekem, John D. K. "Professorial Chair Inaugural Address," *Journal of Mother Tongue Biblical Hermeneutics* 1 (2015a): 158-174.

Ellingworth, Paul and Hatton, Howard A. *UBS Handbook Series: A Handbook on Paul's First Letter to the Corinthians*, Second Edition. New York: United Bible Society, 1994.

Ellis, E. E. "The silenced wives of Corinth (1 Cor. 14:34-35*)*", In *New Testament Textual criticism, its significance for exegesis: Essays in Honour of Bruce M. Metzger*. Oxford: Clarendon Press, 1981.

Fairweather, Janet. "The Epistle to the Galatians and Classical Rhetoric," *TynBul* 45 (1994): 1.

Fee, Gordon and Stuart, Douglas. *How to Read the Bible for all its Worth* 3rd ed. Grand Rapids, MI: Zondervan Publishing House, 1993.

Fee, Gordon. *New Testament Exegesis: A Handbook for Students and Pastors*. Philadelphia: The Westminster Press, 1983.

Fee, Gordon D. *The First Epistle to the Corinthians*. Grand Rapids, MI: Willaim B. Eerdmans Publishing House, 1987.

Gorman, Michael J. *Elements of Biblical Exegesis: A Basic Guide for Students and Ministers*, Revised and Expanded Edition. Grand Rapids, MI: Baker Academic, 2009.

Gowler, David B. "Socio-Rhetorical Interpretation: Textures of a Text and its Reception" in *Journal for the Study of the New Testament* 33(2) (2010): 191-206.

Hager, Chaya Diane. *From Bogota to Madrid to Jerusalem: A Family's Fascinating Journey*. Brookline: Israel Book Shop, 2006.

Homer. *Delphi Complete Works of Homer*. Np: Delphi Classics, 2015.

Jackson, Wayne. "What About the Textus Receptus"? https://www.christiancourier.com/articles/619-what-about-the-textus-receptus [Accessed on 5th February, 2019.

Josephus, Flavius. *The Complete Works* translated by William Whiston. Nashville: Thomas Nelson Inc., 1998.

Jusu, John and Elliott, Matthew. "The Africa Study Bible: God's Word through African Eyes" *Reading the Bible in Context* Issue 2 (2016):4-7.

Kaiser Jr., Walther C. *Toward an Exegetical Theology: Biblical Exegesis for Preaching and Teaching.* Grand Rapids, Michigan: Baker Book House, 1981.

Kuwornu-Adjaottor, J. E. T. "African Biblical Hermeneutics: A Methodology for Mother Tongue Biblical Hermeneutics," *ERATS* 2015 (vol 1) 1-24: 17-18.

Kyei, T. E. "Marriage and Divorce Among the Asante: A study undertaken in the course of the Ashanti Social Survey (1945)" in *Cambridge African Monographs* 14. African Studies Centre, 1992.

Loba-Mkole, Jean-Claude. "Rise of Intercultural Biblical Exegesis in Africa" *HTS* 64(3) 2008 1347-1364.

Lowery, David K. "1 Corinthians" in *The Bible Knowledge Commentary.* Colorado: David C. Cook, 1983.

Lundbom, Jack R. *Jeremiah: A Study in Ancient Hebrew Rhetoric.* 2nd ed.; Winona Lake, Ind.: Eisenbrauns, 1997.

Madipoane, Masenya. "Ruminating on Justin S. Ukpong's Inculturation Hermeneutics and its Implications for the Study of African Biblical Hermeneutics today" *HTS Teologiese Studies/Theological Studies* (2016): 1-6.

Magill, Michael. *New Testament TransLine: A Literal Translation in Outline Format.* Eugene, Oregon: Wipf & Stock, 2002.

Martin, Jobe. T*he Evolution* of a *Creationist.* Texas: Biblical Discipleship Publishers, 2002.

Mathewson, Steven D. *The Art of Preaching Old Testament Narrative* (Grand Rapid, MI: Baker Academics, 2002. https://books.google.com.gh/books?id=xh0HXkcf_TIC&pg=PT4&

Matthews, Victor H. and Moyer, James C. *The Old Testament: Text and Context.* Grand Rapids, MI:Baker Academic, 2012.

Maxey, James A. *From Orality to Orality: A New Paradigm for Contextual Translation of the Bible.* Eugene: Cascade Books, 2009. https://books.google.com.gh/books?id=dflLAwAAQBAJ&pg=PA55&lpg=PA55&dq

Mbiti, J. S. *Bible and Theology in African Christianity.* Oxford: Oxford University Press, 1986.

Mburu, Elizabeth. *African Hermeneutics.* Carlisle: HippoBooks, 2019.

Metzger, Bruce M. *The Bible in Translation Ancient and English Versions.* Grand Rapids: Baker Academic, 2001.

Mickelsen, A. Berkeley. *Interpreting the Bible.* Grand Rapids, MI: Wm. B. Eerdmans Publishing, 1963.

Morris, L. *The Gospel According to Matthew.* Grand Rapids: William B. Eerdmans Publishing Company, 2002.

Muilenburg, James. "Form Criticism and Beyond," *JBL* 88. 1969.

Ossom-Batsa, George. "African Interpretation of the Bible in Communicative Perspective," *Ghana Bulletin of Theology* 2 (2007): 91-104.

Otabil, Mensah. *Beyond the Rivers of Ethiopia: A Biblical Revelation on God's Purpose for the Black Race.* Accra: Altar International, 1992.

Robbins, Vernon K. *Exploring the Texture of Text: A Guide to Socio-Rhetorical Interpretation.* Valley Forge, PA: Trinity Press International, 1996.

Robbins, Vernon K. *Jesus the Teacher: A Socio-Rhetorical Interpretation of Mark*. Philadelphia: Fortress, 1992.

Robbins, Vernon K. "Socio-rhetorical Interpretation," http://www.religion.emory.edu/faculty/robbins/SRI/index.cf

Robbins, Vernon K. *The Invention of Christian Discourse*, I. Blandford Forum, UK: Deo Publishing, 2009.

Robbins, Vernon K. *The Tapestry of Early Christian Discourse: Rhetoric, Society and Ideology*. London and New York: Routledge, 2003.

Robbins, Vernon K. "The We-Passages in Acts and Ancient Sea Voyages" in *Perspectives on Luke-Acts*, ed. C.H. Talbert. Edinburgh: T & T Clark, 1978.

Robertson, A. T. *A Grammar of the Greek New Testament in the Light of Historical Research*. Nashville, TN: Broadman Press, 1934.

Rusbult, Craig. *Worldview*, http://www.asa3.org/ASA/education/views/index.html [Accessed 10 May, 2015]

Sanneh, Lamin (ed). *Translating the Message: The Missionary Impact on Culture*. Maryknoll, New York: Orbis, 2009.

Sanneh, Lamin. "Gospel and Culture: Ramifying Effects of Scripture Translation," in Stine, P.C. ed., *Bible Translation and the Spread of the Church, The Last 200 Years*. Leiden: Brill, 1990.

Schmidt, Peter. *Biblical Measures and their Translation Notes on Translating Biblical Units of Length, Area, Capacity, Weight, Money and Time*. SIL International, 2014.

Shuger, Deborah. "Morris Croll, Flacius Illyricus, and the Origin of Anti-Ciceronianism," *Rhetorica* 3 (1985).

Stott, John R. W. *Baptism and Fullness: The Work of the Holy Spirit Today*, 3rd edition (Leicester: Inter-Varsity Press, 2006.

Strauss, Mark L. *How to Read the Bible in Changing Times: Understanding and Applying God's Word Today*. Grand Rapids, MI: Baker Books, 2011.

Sugirtharajah R.S. *The Bible and the Third World:* Precolonial, Colonial and Postcolonial Encounters. Cambridge: Cambridge University Press, 2001.

Sunukjian, Donald R. "Commentary on Amos" in *The Bible Knowledge Commentary*. Colorado: David C. Cook, 1983.

Tate, W. Randolph. *Handbook for Biblical Interpretation: An Essential Guide to Methods, Terms, and Concepts*. Grand Rapids, MI: Baker Academic, 2012.

The Dead Sea Scrolls Today, rev. ed. Grand Rapids, MI: Eerdmans, 2010.

The Works of Philo Complete Unabridged, trans. C.D. Young, updated ed. Peabody, MA: Hendrickson, 1993.

Thiselton, Anthony C. *Hermeneutics: An introduction*. Grand Rapids, MI: W.B. Eerdmans, 2009.

Tov, Emmanuel. *Textual Criticism of the Hebrew Bible*. Minneapolis: Fortress Press, 2001. Pdf

Traina, Robert A. *Methodical Bible Study*. Grand Rapids, Mi: Zondervan, 1985.

Ukpong, J. S. "Inculturation Hermeneutics: An African Approach to Biblical Interpretation" in D. Walter & L. Ulrich (eds.), *The Bible in a World Context: An Experiment in Contextual Hermeneutics* Grand Rapids, MI: William B. Eerdmans, 2002.

Ukpong, J. S. "Developments in Biblical interpretation in Africa: Historical and hermeneutic directions" in *JTSA* 108 (2000) 3-18.

Ukpong, J. S. "Developments in biblical interpretation in Africa: Historical and hermeneutical directions", in G.O. West & M.W. Dube (eds.), *Bible in Africa, Transactions, Trajectories and Trends* (2001) 11–28, Leiden: Brill.

Ukpong, J. S. "Models and methods on Biblical interpretation in Africa", in *NeueZeitschrift fur Missionswissenschaft* 55 (1999): 279-295.

Ukpong, J. S. "Rereading the Bible with African eyes: Inculturation and Hermeneutics", *JTSA* 41 (1995): 3-14: 9-10.

Ukpong, J. S. "The Parable of the Shrewd Manager (LK 16:1-13): An Essay in the Intercultural Biblical Hermeneutic" *Semeia* 73 (1996): 189-210.

Van Eck, Ernest. "The Word is life: African theology as Biblical and contextual theology," *HTS* 62 (2)2006: 679-701.

Voorwinde, Stephen. "How Normative Is Acts?" in *Vox Reformata* 2010, (33-56'), 39-46.

Waliggo, J. M. et. al., *Inculturation: Its Meaning and Urgency.* Nairobi: St. Paul Publications Africa, 1986.

Waltz, Robert B. *The Encyclopedia of New Testament Textual Criticism.* NP:NP, Ny.

Watson, Duane F. and Hauser, Alan J. *Rhetorical Criticism of the Bible: A Comprehensive Bibliography with Notes on History and Method.* Leiden: New York· Koln, 1994.

West, Gerald. 'On the Eve of an African Biblical Studies: Trajectories and Trends', *JTSA* (1997) 99: 99-115:101.

Wuellner, Wilhelm. "Hermeneutics and Rhetorics: From 'Truth and Method' to 'Truth and Power'" *Scriptura* 3 (1989).

Wuellner, Wilhelm. "Rhetorical Criticism and Its Theory in Culture-Critical Perspective: The Narrative Rhetoric of John 11" in *Text and Interpretation: New Approaches in the Criticism of the New Testament* edited by P. J. Hartin and J. H. Petzer. Leiden: Brill, 1991.

Yaghjian, Lucretia. *Writing Theology Well: A Rhetoric for Theological and Biblical Writers.* New York: Continuum, 2008.

Youngblood, Ronald F. (ed.), *Nelson's Illustrated Bible Dictionary: New and Enhanced Edition.* Nashville: Thomas Nelson, 2014.

Index

A

Acts of the Apostles, iv, xi, 31, 36
Africa, i, v, vii, viii, ix, xi, xii, xv, 1,
   12, 59, 60, 61, 62, 63, 64, 65, 66,
   68, 69, 70, 71, 77, 78, 79, 80, 81,
   84, 85, 86, 87, 88, 92, 99, 102,
   106, 108, 110, 113, 115, 117
African Biblical Studies, iv, viii, xii,
   59, 60, 61, 62, 63, 66, 67, 68, 77,
   87, 109, 111, 113, 117
African Christian Theology, 80,
   111
African context, vii, viii, ix, 59, 61,
   62, 66, 68, 71, 72, 73, 74, 77, 80,
   82, 87, 88, 109
Apocalyptic literature, 40

B

Book context, 21

C

Christianity, ix, xi, xii, xv, 46, 58,
   65, 66, 68, 77, 80, 81, 88, 97, 108,
   113, 114, 115
Church, v, xi, xii, xv, 3, 10, 34, 37,
   44, 65, 79, 81, 82, 88, 89, 99, 100,
   108, 110, 114, 116
Contextual analysis, 17
Contextualization, 72
cultural context, xi, 18, 36, 39, 59,
   70, 74, 76, 109
culture, ix, 2, 17, 18, 33, 39, 46, 50,
   51, 54, 55, 60, 61, 62, 64, 65, 66,
   68, 72, 77, 79, 80, 86, 87, 89, 90,
   91, 99, 106, 108

E

Epistles, iv, xi, 31, 37, 38, 42
exegesis, xi, 1, 2, 3, 4, 5, 7, 13, 15,
   19, 23, 29, 31, 32, 37, 41, 42, 43,
   45, 65, 70, 71, 89, 91, 97, 98, 101,
   108, 109, 110, 111, 114
   diachronic approach, 3
   exegetical, xv, 2, 3, 4, 5, 15, 17,
      21, 29, 31, 34, 36, 41, 42, 57,
      90, 97, 98, 100, 109
   existential approach, 3, 5
   synchronic approach, 3
exegete, xi, 1, 2, 3, 4, 5, 7, 9, 10, 13,
   14, 15, 17, 18, 20, 21, 22, 23, 25,
   26, 27, 28, 29, 31, 36, 37, 39, 40,
   41

G

Gospels, iv, xi, 3, 26, 31, 35, 36, 46,
   82, 84, 105, 109
grammatical units, 25

H

historical context, 17, 19, 34, 39,
   76, 109
Holy Spirit, 4, 5, 22, 37, 61, 99, 105,
   106, 116

I

immediate context, 20, 21, 23, 27, 35, 83
Inculturation, iv, v, 65, 66, 70, 71, 72, 115, 116, 117

L

Law, xi, 31, 32, 33, 42, 100, 113
liberation hermeneutics, 69
Literary context, 2, 20

M

manuscripts, 7, 8, 9, 10, 11, 12
Morphological analysis, 27
morphology, xi, 25, 29
Mother-Tongue Biblical Hermeneutics, v, vii, viii, xii, xv, 79, 85, 89, 109

N

Narrative, xi, 31, 32, 45, 50, 115, 117

P

parables, 36, 91
Part of speech, 28
Poetry, xi, 31
Prophecy, iv, xi, 31, 34, 41
Psalm, 26, 34, 50

R

reactive and apologetic stage, 63
Revelation, xi, 31, 37, 40, 41, 42, 57, 66, 67, 108, 115

S

Scripture, vii, 4, 5, 18, 20, 22, 23, 31, 34, 37, 43, 44, 45, 50, 59, 61, 63, 64, 66, 69, 70, 72, 79, 81, 85, 87, 88, 89, 100, 109, 110, 114, 116
Social context, 18
socio-rhetorical interpretation, xi, xv, 45, 57, 58
  ideological texture, xi, 43, 47, 56, 57
  inner texture, xi, 43, 46, 47, 49, 50, 56, 57
  social and cultural texture, xi, 43, 47, 51, 56, 57
  theological/sacred texture, xi, 43, 47
Syntax, iv, 28

T

Targums, 11, 83, 84
text type, 10, 12
textual criticism, xi, 2, 9, 10, 11, 15, 41
textual variants, 8
Textus Receptus, 8, 114

V

vernacular, 81, 83

W

Wisdom Literature, xi, 31, 62
women leadership, xii, 99

www.ingramcontent.com/pod-product-compliance
Lightning Source LLC
Chambersburg PA
CBHW070335230426
43663CB00011B/2318